Special thanks to
Anne-Rose Schlutbohm
Eryk Fitkau
David & Claudia Monaco (Monaco Reps)
and
Rooney Carruthers
for their professional advice and assistance.

Contents

Contents

Lürzer's Archive Special
200 Best Ad Photographers worldwide 06/07
(ISBN 3-902393-04-1)

Publisher & Editor: Walter Lürzer **Editor-in-chief:** Michael Weinzettl **Associate Editors:** Sonja Hohenthanner, Johanna Krichhammer, Johanna Lang **Project Coordinator:** Sabine Schlager **Layout:** Bernd Biselli **Marketing & Sales Manager:** Sandra Lehnst **Sales Representatives:** Kate Brown, Claudia Coffman, Sheila King, Carina Wicke

Administration/Editorial Office: Lürzer GmbH, Glockmühlstraße 4, 5023 Salzburg, Austria, phone: (43) 662 64 85 85 -0, fax: (43) 662 64 85 85 -60, office@luerzersarchive.com, submission@luerzersarchive.com

Printers: Doosan Corporation, Publishing BG Printing BU, 475-1, Moknae-dong, Danwon-ku, Ansan City, Kyeonggi-Do, Korea 425-100, phone: (82) 31 489 79 36, fax: (82) 31 491 10 47 **Paper:** Matte Art **Pre-Press:** DMSmedia, Fürstenallee 3, 5020 Salzburg, Austria, phone: (43) 662 84 41 95, fax: (43) 662 84 41 95 -95, office@dms-media.at

Submission of material to Lürzer's Archive constitutes representation that the submitter has the authority to grant and grants Lürzer's Archive the right and permission to reproduce, edit and comment editorially on all or any part of the submission in Lürzer's Archive's editorial section. All such reproductions are free of charge to the submitter. Lürzer's Archive assumes no responsibility to return unsolicited material, and reserves the right to accept or reject any advertising material for any reason.

Distributors:
Argentina: *La Paragrafica*, phone: (54) 11 48 15 76 70, tool@paragrafica.com.ar **Australia:** *Selectair Distribution Services*, phone: (61) 2 937 188 66, sales@selectair.com.au **Brazil:** *Livraria Freebook Ltda.*, phone: (55) 11 32 56 05 77, manuel@freebook.com.br; *Casa Ono Com. e Imp. Ltda.*, casaono@uol.com.br; *Open Books*, phone: (55) 48 30 25 77 63, romeu@openbooks.com.br **Bulgaria:** *Milen Marchev*, phone: (359) 2 846 88 32, archive@milenmarchev.com **Canada:** *Keng Seng Enterprises Inc.*, phone: (1) 514 939 39 71, canada@kengseng.com **China:** *Hundred Pages*, phone: (86) 21 540 399 14, jane@hundredpages.com **Costa Rica:** *BAUM S.A.*, phone: (506) 2 53 53 43, baumsa@racsa.co.cr **Czech Republic:** *ADC Czech Republic*, phone: (420) 296 334 850, info@adc-czech.cz **Denmark:** *Tegnecenter*, phone: (45) 33 63 90 33, info@tegnecenter.dk **Egypt:** *Beduinenzelt*, phone: (20) 28 50 32 47, info@beduinenzelt.com **Finland:** *Suomalainen Kirjakauppa*, phone: (358) 10 405 55 52, tom.nordstrom@suomalainenkk.fi **France:** *Lürzer's Archive*, phone: (43) 662 64 85 85 11 (Interlocuteur Français), office@luerzersarchive.com **Germany:** *IPS Datenservice GmbH*, phone: (49) 22 25 7085 334, abo-archiv@ips-datenservice.de **Ghana:** *Chini Productions Ltd.*, phone: (233) 21 51 54 98, archive@chiniproductions.com **Greece:** *Studio Bookshop*, phone: (30) 21 03 60 06 47, office@studiobookshop.com **Hong Kong:** *Keng Seng Trading & Co. Ltd.*, phone: (852) 25 91 10 68, lawrence@kengseng.com **Hungary:** *Librotrade Kft.*, phone: (36) 12 54 02 61, periodicals@librotrade.hu **India:** *IBD*, phone: (91) 22 22 82 52 20, ibd@ vsnl.com; *SBD*, phone: (91) 11 28 71 41 38, sbds@bol.net.in **Indonesia:** *Basheer Graphic Books*, abdul@basheergraphic.com **Italy:** *Ellesette*, phone: (39) 011 8 98 07 66, ellesette@ellesette.com; *RED*, phone: (39) 059 21 27 92, info@redonline.it **Japan:** *Yohan Inc.*, phone: (81) 3 57 86 74 23, magazine@yohan.co.jp **Korea:** *Yi Sam Sa*, phone: (82) 27 35 30 02, yss23k@kornet.net **Malaysia:** *How & Why Sdn. Bhd.*, phone: (60) 3 78 77 48 00, info@howwwhy.com; *The Other Bookstore*, phone: (60) 19 238 85 87, hajaotherbookstore@yahoo.com **Mexico:** *Rolando de la Piedra*, phone: (52) 52 57 18 17, hosrpb@prodigy.net.mx **Netherlands/Belgium:** *Bruil & Van de Staaij*, phone: (31) 522 26 13 03, info@bruil.info **New Zealand:** *Mercury Subs. Ltd.*, phone: (64) 9 979 25 60, subs@mercurysubs.co.nz **Nigeria:** *Chini Productions*, phone: (234) 1 723 2813, archive@chiniproductions.com **Norway:** *Luth & Co/Font Shop*, phone: (47) 23 28 76 30, info@luth.no **Philippines:** *Roger Pe*, rbpe@ddbphil.com **Poland:** *VFP Communications*, kehrt@media.com.pl **Portugal:** *Marka Lda.*, phone: (351) 213 22 40 40, apoio.clientes@marka.pt; *Tema Lda.*, belmiro@mail.telepac.pt **Romania:** *Rospotline*, phone: (40) 21 311 70 99, diana@rospotline.com **Russia:** *Index Design*, info@indexdesign.ru; *IndexMarket*, phone: (7) 095 158 63 10, info@indexmarket.ru **Singapore:** *Basheer Graphic Books*, phone: (65) 63 36 08 10, abdul@basheergraphic.com; *Page One*, phone: (65) 67 42 2088, pageone@singnet.com.sg **Slovakia:** *Archive F.K.*, phone: (42) 1 90 5620 538, archivefk@luerzersarchive.com **Slovenia/Albania/Bosnia & Herzegovina/Croatia/Macedonia/Serbia & Montenegro:** *New Moments D.O.O.*, phone: (386) 1 420 19 51, ideas@newmoment.si **South Africa:** *International Subscription Services*, phone: (27) 11 782 22 23, isscc@icon.co.za **Spain:** *Comercial Atheneum S.A.*, phone: (34) 93 6 54 40 61, suscri.bcn@atheneum.com; *Promotora De Prensa*, phone: (34) 93 2 45 14 64; *Publitrade*, phone: (34) 91 567 10 30, gruptrad@gruptrad.net **Sweden:** *Svenska Interpress*, info@interpress.se **Taiwan:** *Far Go Chen Co. Ltd.*, phone: (886) 2 27 04 31 18, fargo899@ms35.hinet.net **Thailand:** *B2S Co. Ltd.*, phone: (66) 29 25 63 00, YiSorrapong@b2s.co.th **Turkey:** *Alternatif*, phone: (90) 212 217 73 63, alternatif@grafikkitaplari.com; *Evrensel*, phone: (90) 21 23 56 72 76, evrensely@superonline.com **Ukraine:** *DAN*, phone: (38) 056 798 34 40, olga@ceo.com.ua **United Arab Emirates/Bahrein/Kuwait/Oman/Saudi Arabia/Qatar:** *MBR Bookshop LLC*, phone: (971) 43 96 41 41, asoni@emirates.net.ae **United Kingdom/Ireland:** *Central Books*, phone: (44) 20 85 25 88 25, sasha@centralbooks.com; *Timscris*, phone: (44) 20 8877 7920, kb@luerzersarchive.com **Uruguay:** *Graffiti S.R.L.*, phone: (598) 29 00 62 45, graffiti@fastlink.com.uy **United States:** *Showcase, Archive, Inc.*, phone: (1) 800 989 94 94, archive@cambeywest.com **Venezuela:** *Gilberto Cardenas*, phone: (58) 02 902 92 95, g_cardenas2@yahoo.com **Vietnam:** *Chim Cau Shop*, phone: (848) 914 35 72, hoangtrang@chimcau.com.vn

All other countries: *IPS*, Meckenheim, Germany, phone: (49) 22 25 70 85 334 (English speaking), email: sub-archive@ips-datenservice.de

How to use your Archive:
Guide to symbols: : Advertising Agency : Art Director : Copywriter : Photographer : Client : Modelmaker : Illustrator : Typographer : Production Company : Director

All editorial material reproduced in Lürzer's Archive Special are categorized by product, e.g. "Animals." Product groups are shown alphabetically. Every editorial page is cross-referenced with an Archive number, the first two digits indicating the year in which the special was published, and the second three digits being continuous page numbers for that particular product group. For example, 200bph 06.001 under "Animals" indicates the Volume published in 2006, and page 1 of that product group.

Cover page:
: Jonathan Kantor : Self-promotion

Profusion of up-and-coming talent makes for a fascinating mix of new and more familiar names

One of the more surprising – yet exhilarating – aspects of the collection of advertising photographers whose work is to be admired on the following pages is the fact that about one half of them will be familiar to you from the previous volume, 200 Best Ad Photographers worldwide 04/05, while the other half are "newcomers" – to this biennial publication, at least. You won't, in other words, be getting a recycled version of the same old bunch of names and faces, and can, in fact, look forward to a volume offering lots of potential for new and exciting discoveries.

This is chiefly due to the selection criteria employed:

1. Every photographer featured in this volume had to be recommended by an agency art director. This fact alone means that many of those submitting proposals might have changed their "favorite" photographers over the course of the past two years – or may have simply thought that an up-and-coming talent was so good they deserved to have their work featured in the 200 Best collection. In all, some 600 photographers were nominated by these art directors from top ad agencies worldwide, yet less than one third of this total actually made it into this volume.

2. If not recommended by an art director, a photographer's work must have previously appeared in an Archive publication. This selection criterion, too, tended to favour the inclusion of new and interesting talents.

3. Only commercial work published during the past 18 months was eligible. Galling though this may have been for some photographers whose brilliant work we were able to showcase in 200 Best Ad Photographers worldwide 04/05, if the work from these past 18 months – calculated from the time when selection began – was not up to snuff (due either to their own failings or because they were working with a client/agency that allowed them little or no creative freedom), they, too, will find that they did not make the grade for inclusion in the 200 Best Ad Photographers worldwide 06/07.

A comparison of the breakdown of photographers by individual country with the figures from our last issue of 200 Best reveals that there have not been all that many changes. The top-ranking country, the US, boasts almost the same number of photographers in this volume, namely 37, as opposed to 35 in the previous one. Germany, though still in third place, now has 15 photographers, down from the 27 featured in the 04/05 issue. Countries such as South Africa and New Zealand on the other hand, which had just one photographer in the previous volume, have now edged their way up to five and three, respectively.

External experts provided the additional discernment required when completing the final selection process. They included Anne-Rose Schlutbohm, the former publisher of "Profession Photographe," Paris, David and Claudia Monaco from Monaco Reps, New York, and Sydney-based photographer Eryk Fitkau. We should like to take this opportunity to express our sincere appreciation to them all for their invaluable input in the compiling of the work featured in this volume.

A total of 20,000 copies of 200 Best Ad Photographers worldwide 06/07 will be circulated to art buyers throughout the world by our distributors based in no less than 35 different countries.

We shall also be mailing out 15 copies on behalf of each photographer featured in 200 Best Ad Photographers worldwide, and each will also be represented by a Personal Showcase at www.luerzersarchive.com, enabling them to upload 12 selected images of their own best work to a website boasting 15 million hits and 150,000 visitors per month.

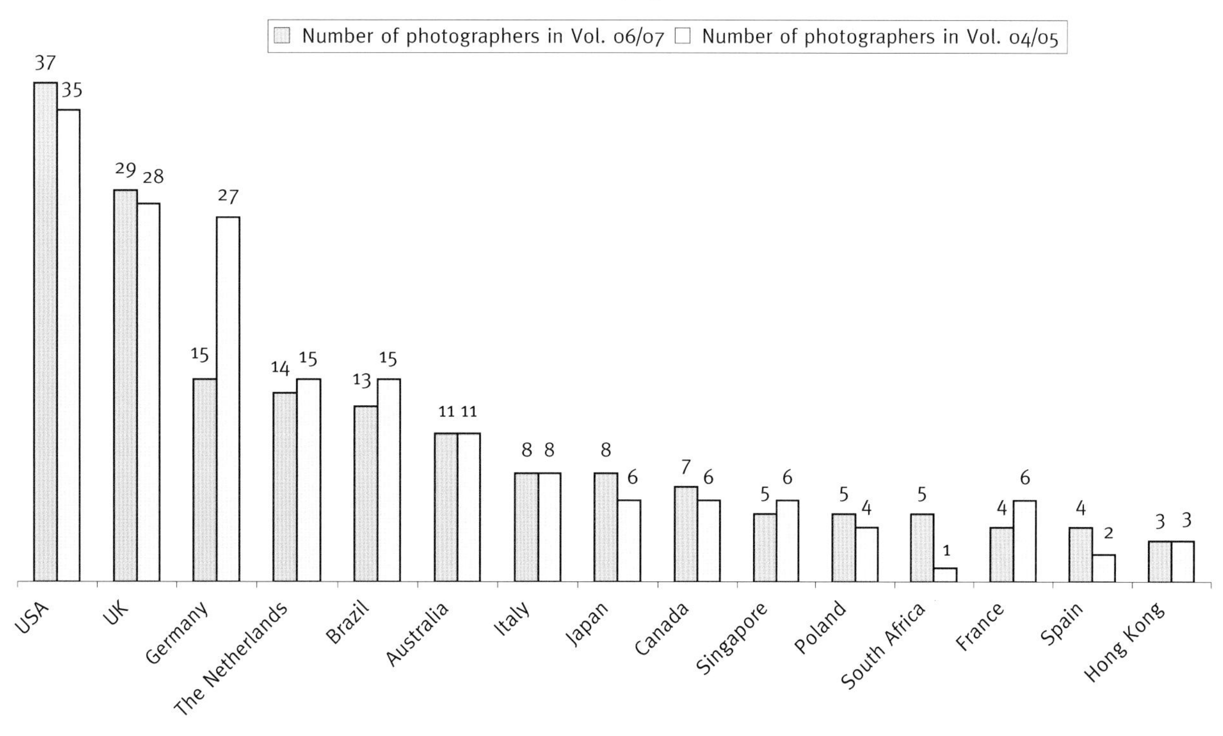

There are still wars, there are still fashion designers

Rooney Carruthers has been described as one of the most inspiring creative directors in the business. He has been an art director at such top London agencies as BMP and BBH, later moving on to WCRS as Creative Director and, before going on to co-found the VCCP agency, also working as Executive Creative Director at FCB in San Francisco. Over the years, his campaigns for brands such as Courage, Olivio, Levi's, Caffrey's, and BMW have won numerous advertising awards, yet there is one in particular that stands out: the Häagen-Dazs campaign, created with his copywriting partner Larry Barker at BBH in the early 90s, is considered one of the all-time advertising industry landmarks and a shining example of a successful cooperation between an art director and a photographer. Michael Weinzettl spoke to Rooney Carruthers about advertising photography.

L.A.: What, to you, is a good advertising photo?
Rooney Carruthers: One that stops you in your tracks.
L.A.: What qualities does a good advertising photographer need?
Rooney Carruthers: Patience and enthusiasm.
L.A.: What is the role of the advertising photographer?
Rooney Carruthers: To make a concept a beautiful reality.
L.A.: Whose work in the history of photography do you admire most?
Rooney Carruthers: That of Jeanloup Sieff.
L.A.: Why is it that brilliant photographers frequently don't produce their best work in advertising?
Rooney Carruthers: Because they don't own the concept, they don't necessarily have creative freedom.
L.A.: What have been some of the most fruitful collaborations between you, as an art director, and a photographer?
Rooney Carruthers: Several years ago now, I did the Häagen-Dazs campaign. We were looking at various photographers to shoot for a very sensuous feel. I must have seen at least twenty photographers until, finally, I decided to meet Jeanloup Sieff. I flew to Paris and we met for lunch. I was at BBH at the time. I went on my own, and Jeanloup and I just chatted. It was very brave of my creative director – John Hegarty – to let me do this, but that's John's way! The photographs needed to quietly smoulder. We went for a soft feel, almost like a 1930s Hollywood portrait of a starlet. Jeanloup is, to my mind, the Renoir of fashion photography. Only he could photograph the hairs on a girl's neck and make you want to kiss her! In his studio, he just raised a piece of black velvet, took out his Hasselblad and did what he was best at: making women look and feel as natural as mother's milk!
L.A.: What's your idea of an ideal collaboration between an art director and a photographer?
Rooney Carruthers: Generally, until a pre-prod meeting, creatives hold back on meeting people. We look at books with our art buyers and choose three, obviously one of them being a preference. We then send the work out and see if the photographers are interested – and, of course, available. I choose a photographer primarily on his work and reputation. And, of course, if we've "clicked" in the pre-production meeting. Remember that the creative has probably worked on the ad for three months, then gone through client approval, budgets and research. So, at this point, his job should be fun! What I don't want is to work with a pumped-up, pain-in-the-arse prima donna! If a photographer is like this, we just won't collaborate.
L.A.: What, for you, are some of the trends in recent photography?
Rooney Carruthers: Architecture seems to have taken on a new form of fashion. Location is everything these days.
L.A.: Has digital photography revolutionized photography? Has it made photography in general more "democratic"?
Rooney Carruthers: I totally agree. Everyone around the camera gets to see the image as soon as it's snapped and, through their Apple Macs, are comping pictures together on-set. A lot better than the old Polaroids.

L.A.: Do you think we have become oversaturated with images and that, as a result, the power of photography – the power of images – has declined, or is about to decline?
Rooney Carruthers: No, there are still wars, there are still fashion designers, and there is still poverty and more creativity than before. They all use the power of photography.
L.A.: Can you think of a recent photographic image that has struck you in an extraordinary fashion, one that immediately comes to mind?
Rooney Carruthers: A mother and son fleeing danger in Israel yesterday, front cover of The Independent 24/07/06.
L.A.: If you could choose to have your portrait taken by anyone at all in the history of photography, who would that be?
Rooney Carruthers: Irving Penn, because I'd like to be in his V-shaped set, sitting in a chair where hundreds of famous people have been so perfectly put on film forever.

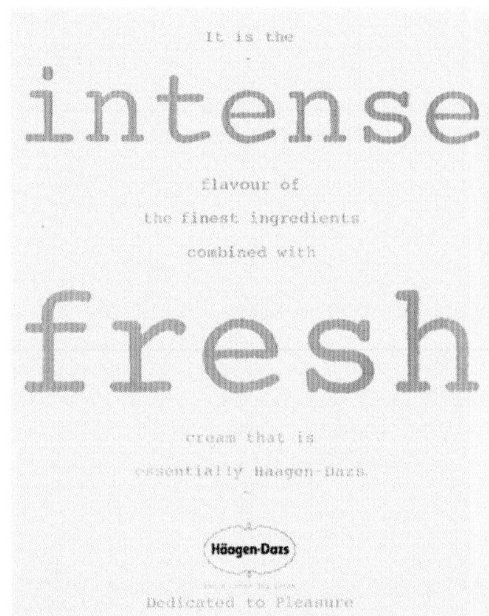

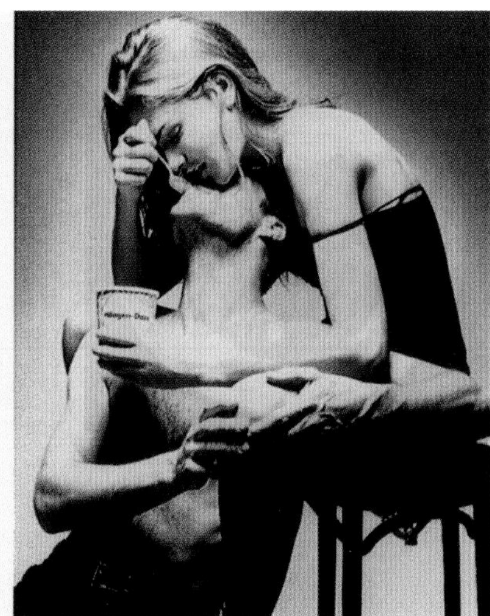

First appeared in 1991. : Bartle Bogle Hegarty, London : Rooney Carruthers : Larry Barker : Jeanloup Sieff

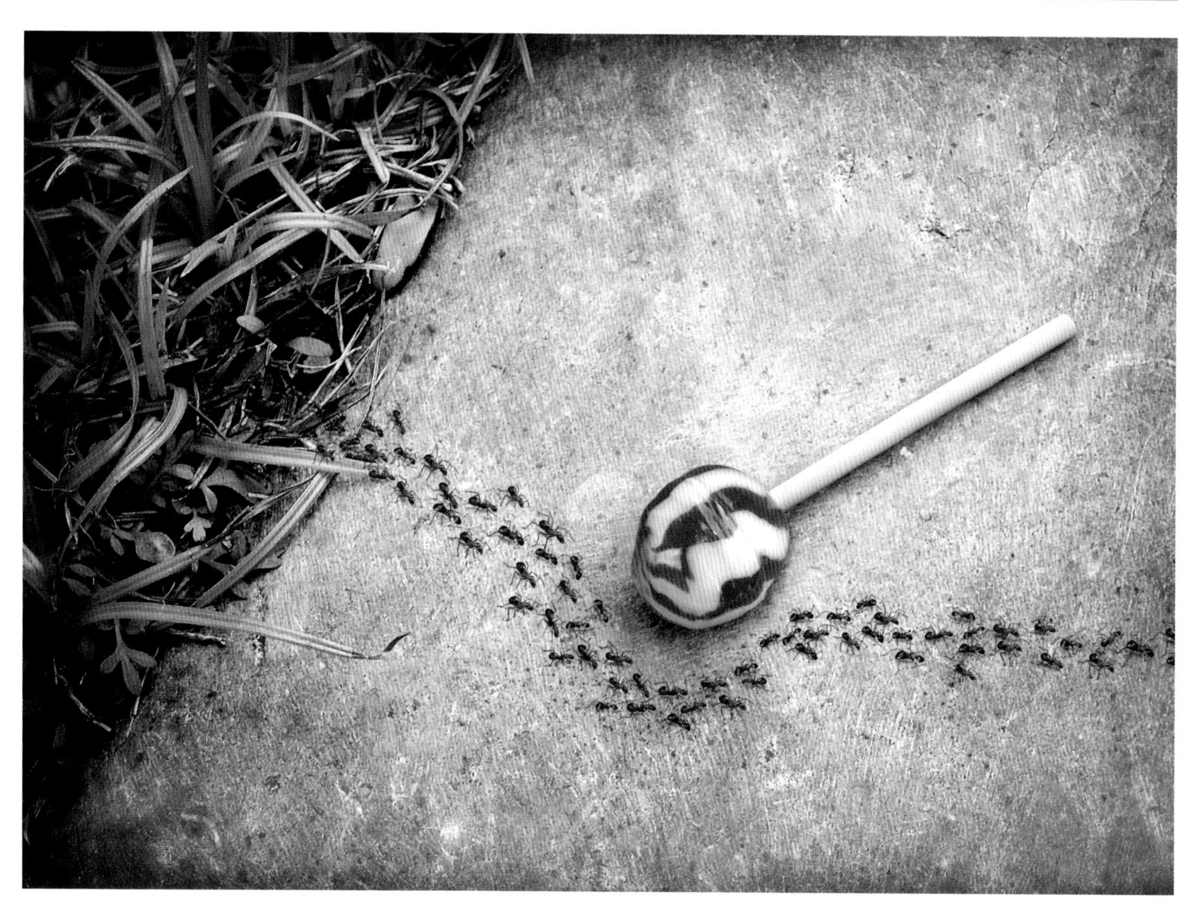

📷: Ramón Serrano A: DDB, Barcelona ✎: Bernat Sanroma ♔: Chupa Chups

📷: Sebastian Siah A: Bates Asia, Singapore ✎: Swee Ling Ng ♔: WOMAD

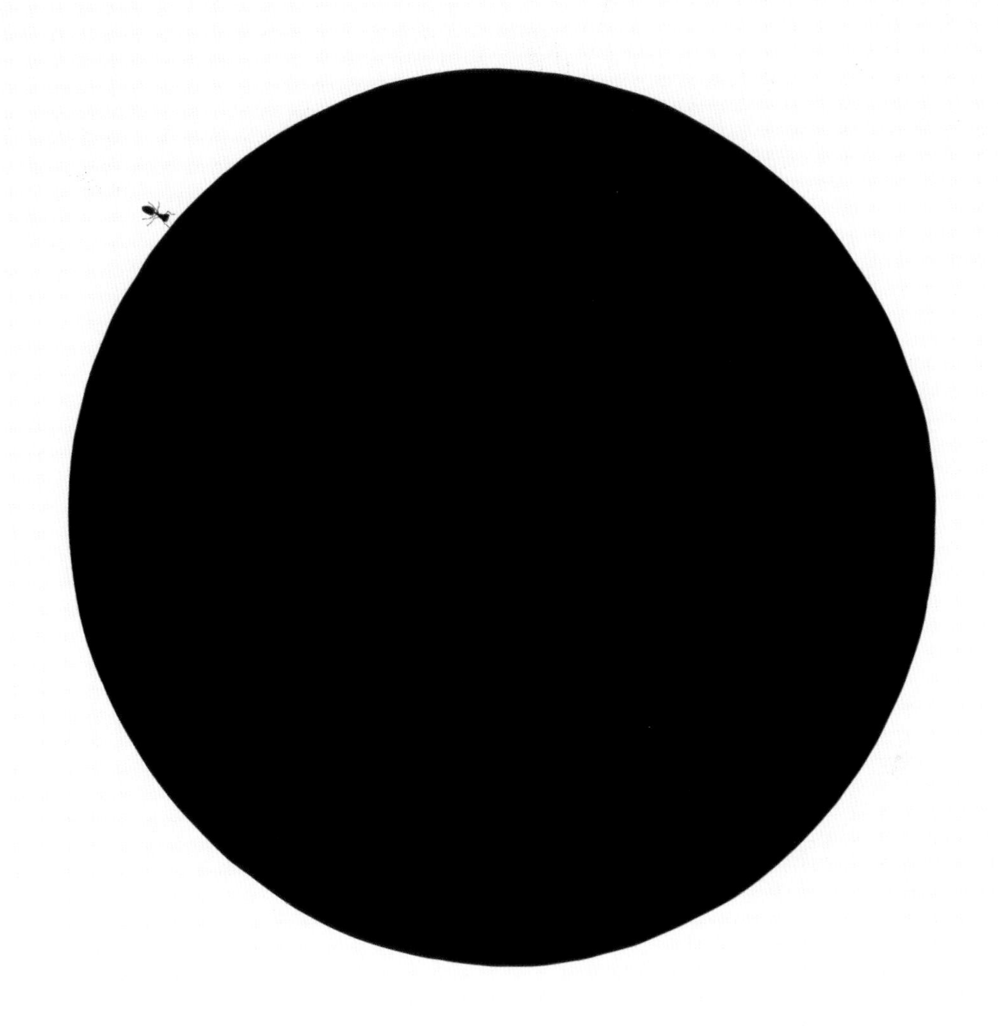

📷: Kenji Aoki A: Shiseido In-house, Tokyo ✏: Noria Nakamura ♕: Shiseido

[camera icon]: Mark Laita [agency icon]: Los Angeles County Museum of Natural History In-house [pen icon]: Lauren Delgadillo [client icon]: Los Angeles County Museum of Natural History

📷: Philip Rostron A: Extension Marketing, Toronto ✎: Charles Bongers ♕: National Bank Financial

📷: Chris Budgeon A: Badjar, Melbourne ✏: Greg Edwards ♕: Foster's

[camera icon]: William Huber [pen icon]: Jennifer L., Martin Laski [crown icon]: Centurion

: Fulvio Bonavia : D'Adda, Lorenzini, Vigorelli, BBDO, Milan : Serena Di Bruno : Perlana

📷: Fulvio Bonavia A: Red Cell, Milan ✎: Giorgio Cignoni ♔: Yamaha Motor

📷: Gerard Turnley A: Net#work BBDO, Johannesburg ✎: Thomas Cullinan ♛: Designer Group

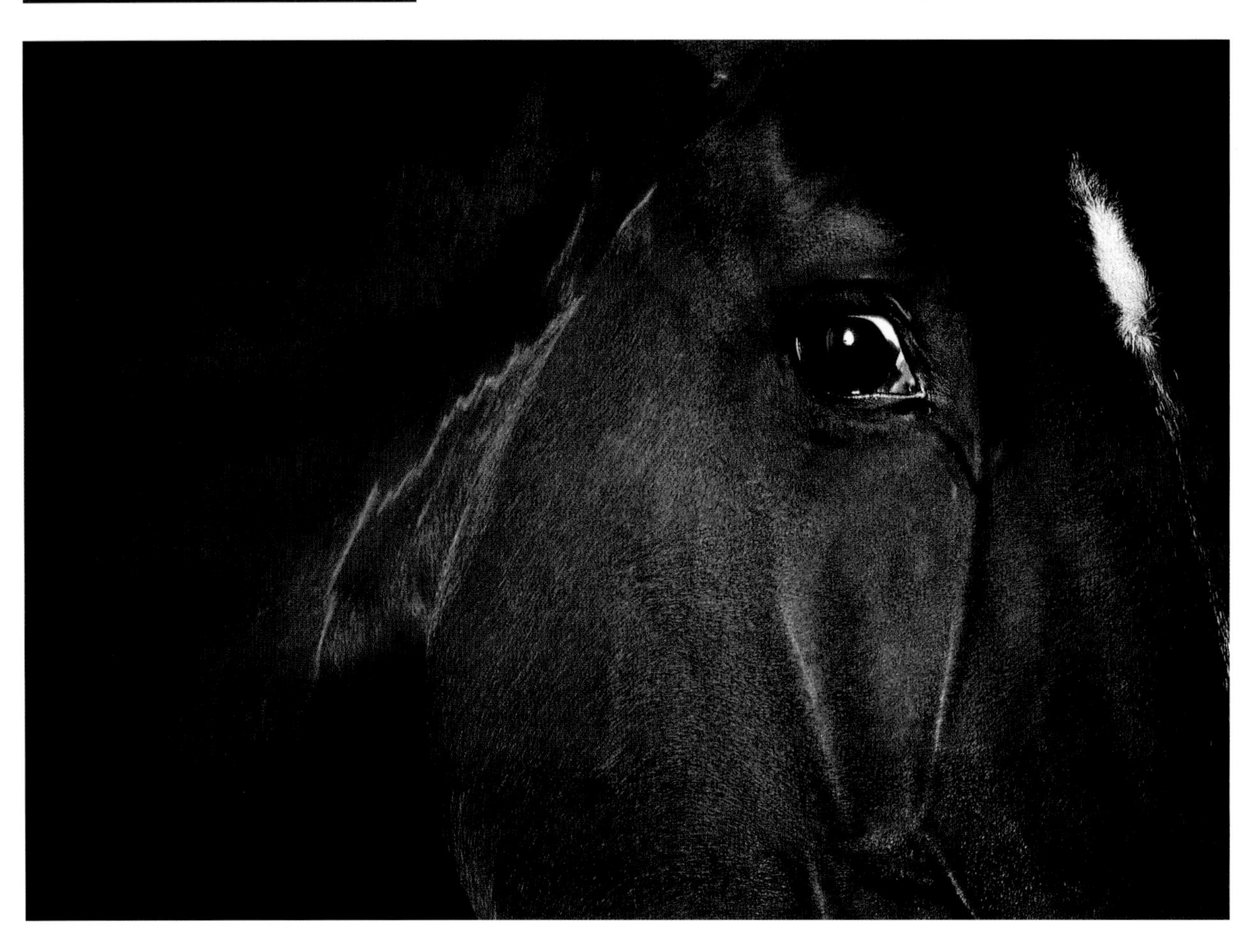

📷: Winkler & Noah ✎: Hilde Capra ♔: Hilde Capra

📷: Guy Neveling ♔: Self-promotion

: David Stewart : Has Design, London : Marcus Haslam, Wesley West : Self-promotion

: Sebastian Siah : Bates Asia, Singapore : Swee Ling Ng : WOMAD

📷: Paulo Mancini A: F/Nazca Saatchi & Saatchi, São Paulo ✎: Alexandre Pagano ♛: Arno

📷: Mark Laita A: Vitro Robertson, San Diego, California ✎: Bill Stowe ♛: Asics

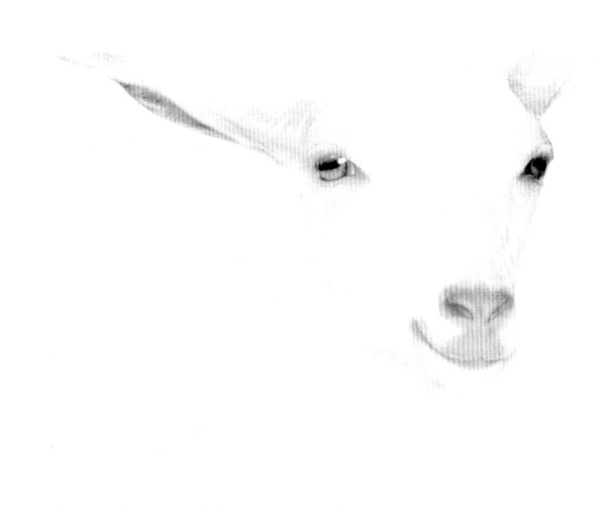

📷: Andrea Melcangi ⌂: JWT, Milan ✎: Fabio Anzani ♔: Ente Nazionale Protezione Animali

📷: George Simhoni A: Cossette, Montreal ✎: Rene-Michel Vachon ♕: Dairy Farmers of Canada

📷: Glen Wexler A: The Richards Group, Dallas ✎: Linsey Parks ♕: Chick-fil-A

📷: Jim Erickson A: The Richards Group, Dallas ✎: Todd Tucker ♛: Chick-fil-A

📷: Garry Simpson A: TBWA, Paris ✏: Chris Garbutt ♔: Pedigree

📷: Markku Lahdesmaki A: Bob Helsinki, Helsinki ▭: Jon Granstrom ♔: Aamulehti

📷: Stuart Hall A: Grey Worldwide, Düsseldorf, Germany ✎: Sebastian Kaiser ♛: Grohe

📷: Andreas Smetana A: Leo Burnett, Sydney ✎: Michael Spirkovski ♛: World Wildlife Fund

📷: William Huber A: Cole & Weber/Red Cell, Seattle ✎: Travis Britton ♛: Venge Vineyards

[camera]: Scheffold.Vizner [agency]: Jung von Matt/ Limmat, Zurich [art director]: Michael Rottmann [client]: Granador

: Michael Schnabel : CCA, Irvine, California : Lovemando : Samsung

: Kai-Uwe Gundlach : Ringzwei, Hamburg : Dirk Linke : BMW

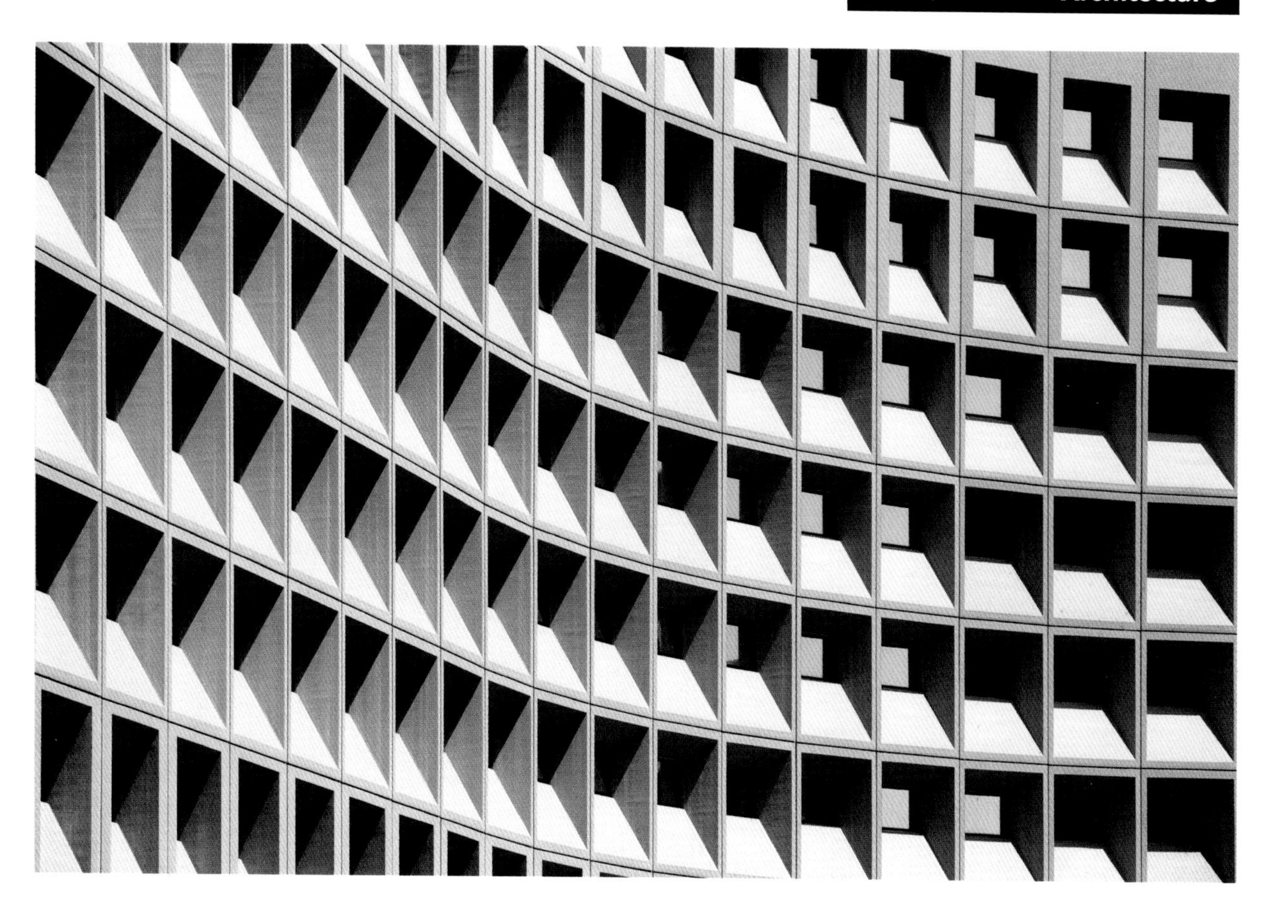

📷: George Apostolidis ▭: Jill Kluge ♔: Mandarin Oriental Hotel

📷: Michael Schnabel ⌂: CCA, New York ✏: Ann Losquadro 👑: Samsung

📷: Markku Lahdesmaki 👑: Self-promotion

[camera icon]: Anthony Redpath [crown icon]: Self-promotion

📷: David Allan Brandt A: Team/Young & Rubicam, Dubai ✎: Komal Bedi, Sam Ahmed ♔: Emaar

📷: Marcelo Coelho A: VC Editorial, Belo Horizonte, Brazil ✎: Valter Costa ♔: The State Government of Minas Gerais

📷: David Allan Brandt ✎: Ure Design, San Francisco ✍: Alyssa Ure, David Allan Brandt ♛: Norman Maslov

[camera icon]: Rolph Gobits [A icon]: The Richards Group, Dallas [pencil icon]: Lynda Hodge [crown icon]: Sotheby's

: Garry Simpson : M&C Saatchi, London : Bill Gallacher : British Airways

📷: Andy Glass A: McCann Erickson, London ✏: Brett O'Connor ♛: GlaxoSmithKline

📷: Andy Glass A: TBWA, Paris ♛: Nissan

: Harry De Zitter : TBWA, Hong Kong : Darius Tang : Shangri-La Hotels & Resorts

: Andy Glass : TBWA, Paris : Sophie Guyon : Absolut Vodka

📷: Kai-Uwe Gundlach A: KW 43, Düsseldorf, Germany ✎: Margit Tabert ♔: Porsche Design

📷: Nick Meek A: McCann Erickson, London ✏: Mark Reddy ♕: American Airlines

📷: Sean Izzard A: Saatchi & Saatchi, Sydney ✏: Andy Dilallo, Jay Benjamin ♕: Olympus

: Geir Florhaug

: Boudewijn Smit : McCann, Oslo : Espen Lie Andersen : Statoil

📷: Pete Seaward 👑: Self-promotion

📷: Christian Stoll A: Ogilvy & Mather, New York ✏: Michael Paterson ♛: IBM

📷: Robert Wilson A: Enterprise IG, London ✎: Tim Brennan ♔: Credit Suisse

📷: Jaap Vliegenthart A: Euro RSCG, Amsterdam ✎: Bert Kerkhof ♕: Citroën

KOST

: Dirk Karsten : FoxCompany, Brescia, Italy : Francesco Lucca : Platek

📷: Johann Sebastian Hänel A: Jung von Matt/Neckar, Stuttgart, Germany ✎: Tobias Eichinger ♕: EnBW

: Stuart Hall A: Arnold Worldwide, Washington D.C. : Robert Petkofsky : Amtrak

: Simon Mills A: TBWA, London : Phil Martin : Eurostar

📷: Edo Kars A: Gr8 Films, Amsterdam ✎: Gideon Rijnders ♔: Fotoformation

: Blinkk : CDD, London : Dave Dye : Mercedes-Benz

📷: Darran Rees A: TBWA\Chiat\Day, Los Angeles ✎: Chris Lynch ♔: Nissan

📷: Thomas L. Fischer ✎: Oliver Klyne ♛: Novum – World of Graphic Design

: Andreas Mädler

: Ivo von Renner : Springer & Jacoby, Hamburg : Gerrit Zinke : Mercedes-Benz

: Fulvio Bonavia : Armando Testa, Turin : Mendibil Aniana Pagani : Lancia

: Garry Simpson : Rainey Kelly Campbell Roalfe/Y&R, London : Jerry Hollens : Land Rover

: Simon Stock : Publicis, Dallas : Eric Moncaleano : BMW

: Simon Stock : JWT, Houston, Texas : Bob Braun : Shell

: Glen Wexler : Saatchi & Saatchi, Los Angeles : Mark Taylor : Toyota

: Ramón Serrano : DDB, Barcelona : Xavier Solé : Audi

: Florian Geiss : Journal International, Munich : Martin Kreuzer : Amex

: Rainer Stratmann : RPA, Los Angeles : Tatum Cardillo, Joe Baratelli : Honda

📷: Dirk Karsten A: Saatchi & Saatchi, Rome ✏: Francesca Avella ♛: Platek

📷: Michael Schnabel A: BBDO, Detroit ✏: Paul Szary ♛: Jeep

: Bo Hylén : Goodby, Silverstein & Partners, San Francisco : Michael Fiore : Saturn

: George Simhoni : Self-promotion

📷: Ljubodrag Andric A: Grip, Toronto ✎: Alan Madill ♛: Honda

📷: Ljubodrag Andric A: Grey, Toronto ✎: David Rhodes ♛: Trimark

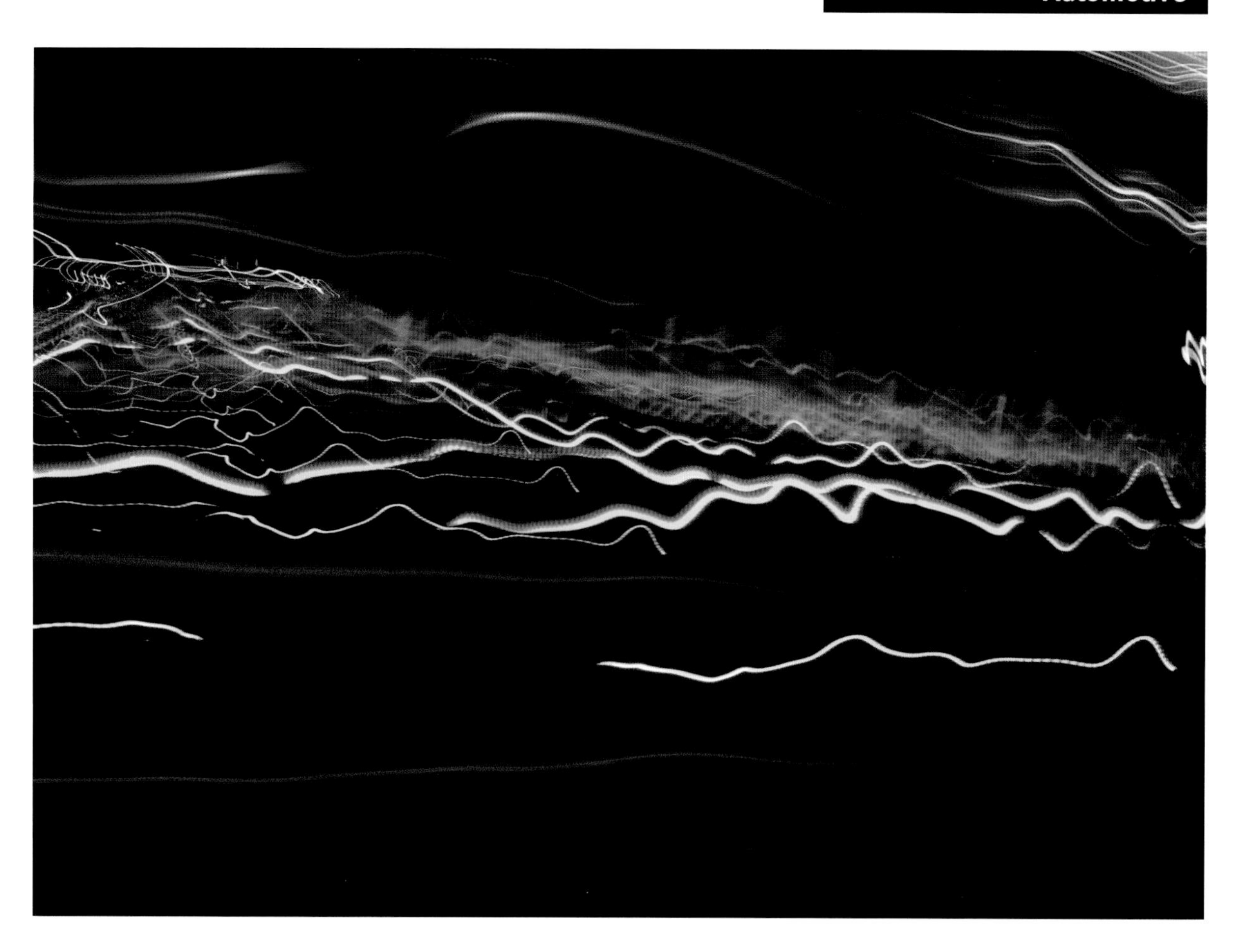

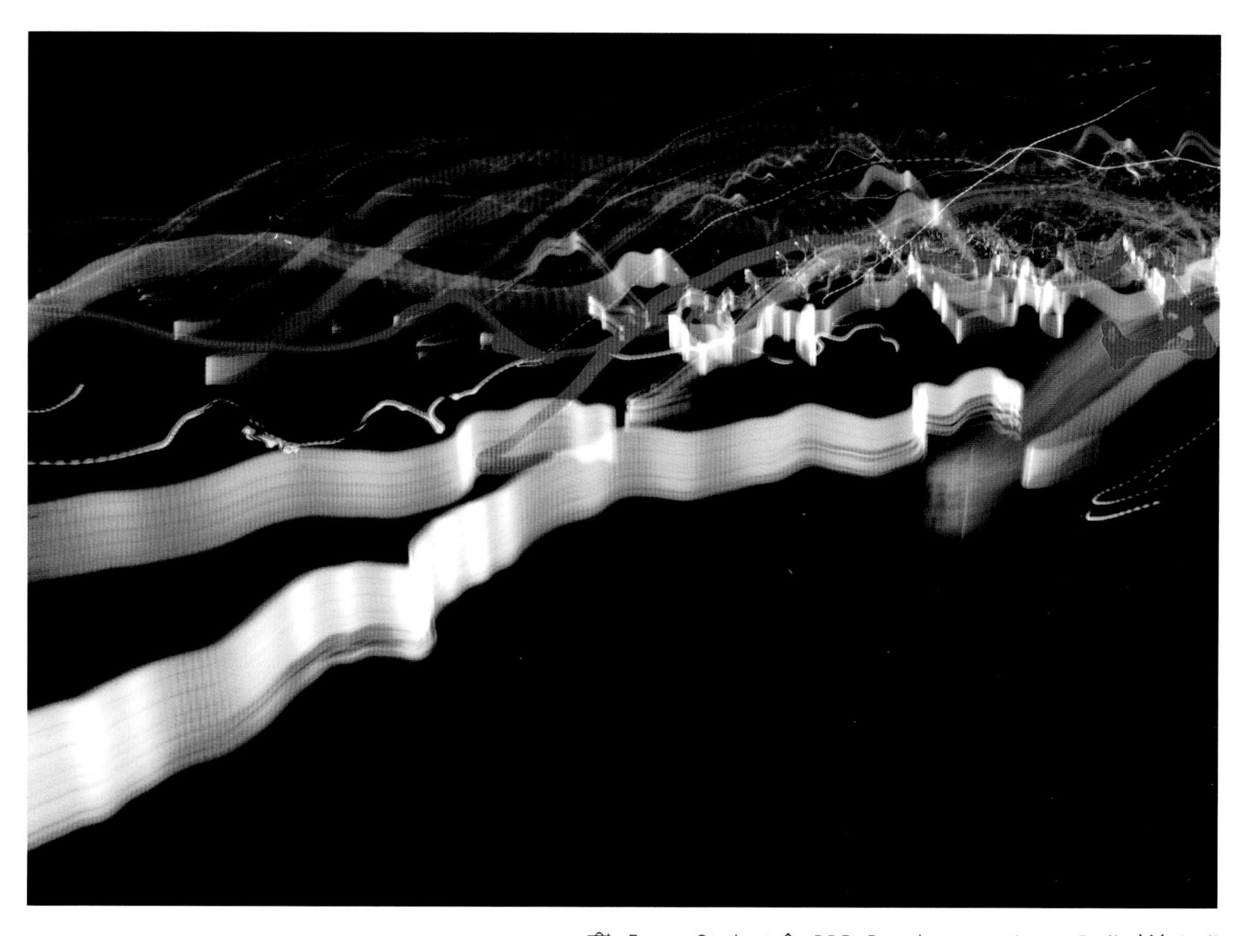

📷: Fergus Stothart A: DDB, Barcelona ▭: Jaume Badia ♕: Audi

: Richard Prescott : Saddington & Baynes In-house, London : Richard Prescott, Clive Booth : Saddington & Baynes

: Ricardo Miras : DDB, Barcelona : Jaume Badia : Audi

: Anton Watts : Interone Worldwide, Munich : Shin Oh : BMW

: Nadav Kander : DDB, London : Nick Allsop : Volkswagen

: Tim Damon : Crispin Porter + Bogusky, Miami : Tony Calcao : MINI

: Tim Damon : Campbell-Ewald, Detroit : Jen Liva : Chevrolet

: Tim Damon : The Designory, Long Beach, California : Mike Monley : Nissan

📷: Tim Damon A: Springer & Jacoby, London ▭: Ben Carratu ♕: Mercedes-Benz

📷: Tim Damon A: E-Graphics, Tokyo ♕: Nissan

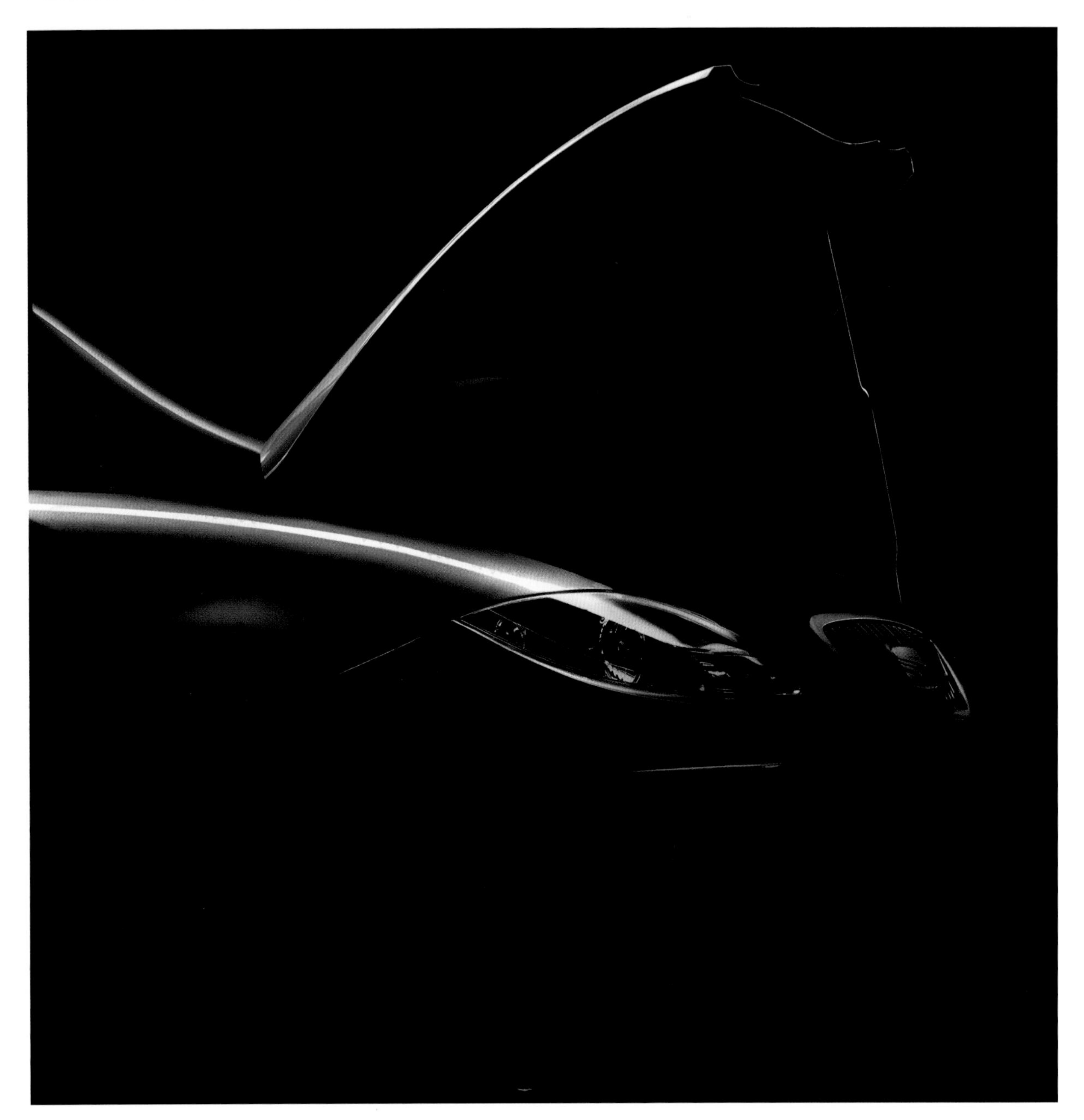

📷: Ramón Serrano A: Atletico International, Barcelona ✎: Michele Salati ♛: Seat

📷: RJ Muna A: Young & Rubicam, Los Angeles ▭: Trisha Ting ♕: Jaguar

: Uwe Düttmann : Kemper Trautmann, Hamburg : Gerrit Zinke : Audi

[camera icon]: Uwe Düttmann [pen icon]: Dirk Linke [crown icon]: BMW Magazine

: Peter Keil : DaimlerChrysler

: Cédric Delsaux : BETC Euro RSCG, Paris : Remy Tricot : Peugeot

📷: Jan Willem Scholten 👑: Self-promotion

📷: Jan Willem Scholten A: Typoweb, Paris 👑: Nissan

📷: Simon Warmer A: Eigen Fabrikaat, Amsterdam ▭: Peter Scholtens ♕: AutoTrack.nl

📷: Joris van Velzen 👑: Mercury

📷: Glen Wexler 👑: Natural Health Magazine

📷: Florian Geiss A: Saatchi & Saatchi, Vienna ✎: Michael Kaiser 👑: Mobilkom Austria

: Eryk Fitkau : Dentsu, Singapore : Ginny Chan : Canon

: Eryk Fitkau : E. Productions, Melbourne : Eryk Fitkau : Croce Colosimo

📷: Andreas Smetana A: M&C Saatchi, Sydney ✎: Chris Round ♔: Audi

[camera icon]: Christophe Gilbert [A icon]: LG&F, Brussels [pen icon]: Benoit Hilson [crown icon]: BEKA

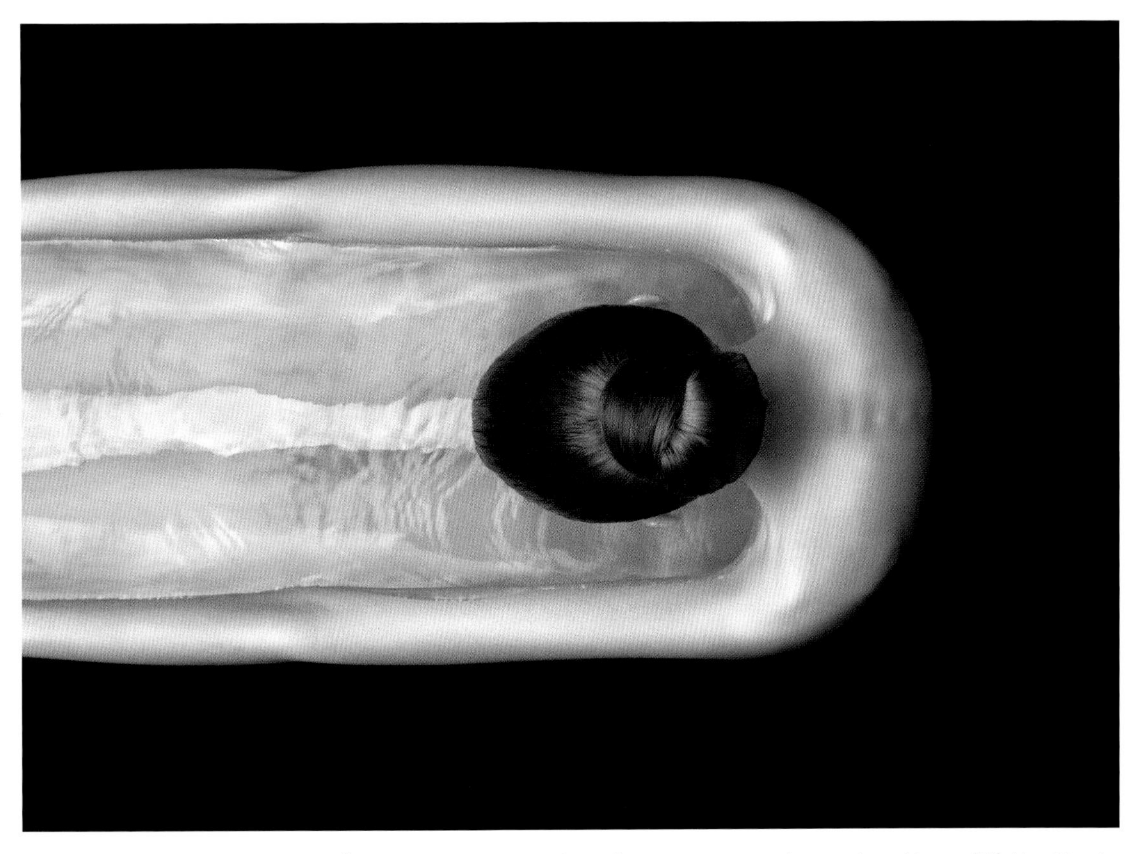

[camera icon]: Christophe Gilbert [A icon]: GV\Company, Brussels [pen icon]: Ivan Moons [crown icon]: Van Marcke

📷: David Allan Brandt A: Grey Worldwide, Beijing ✏: Chee Guan Yue, Sam Shen 👑: Mercedes-Benz

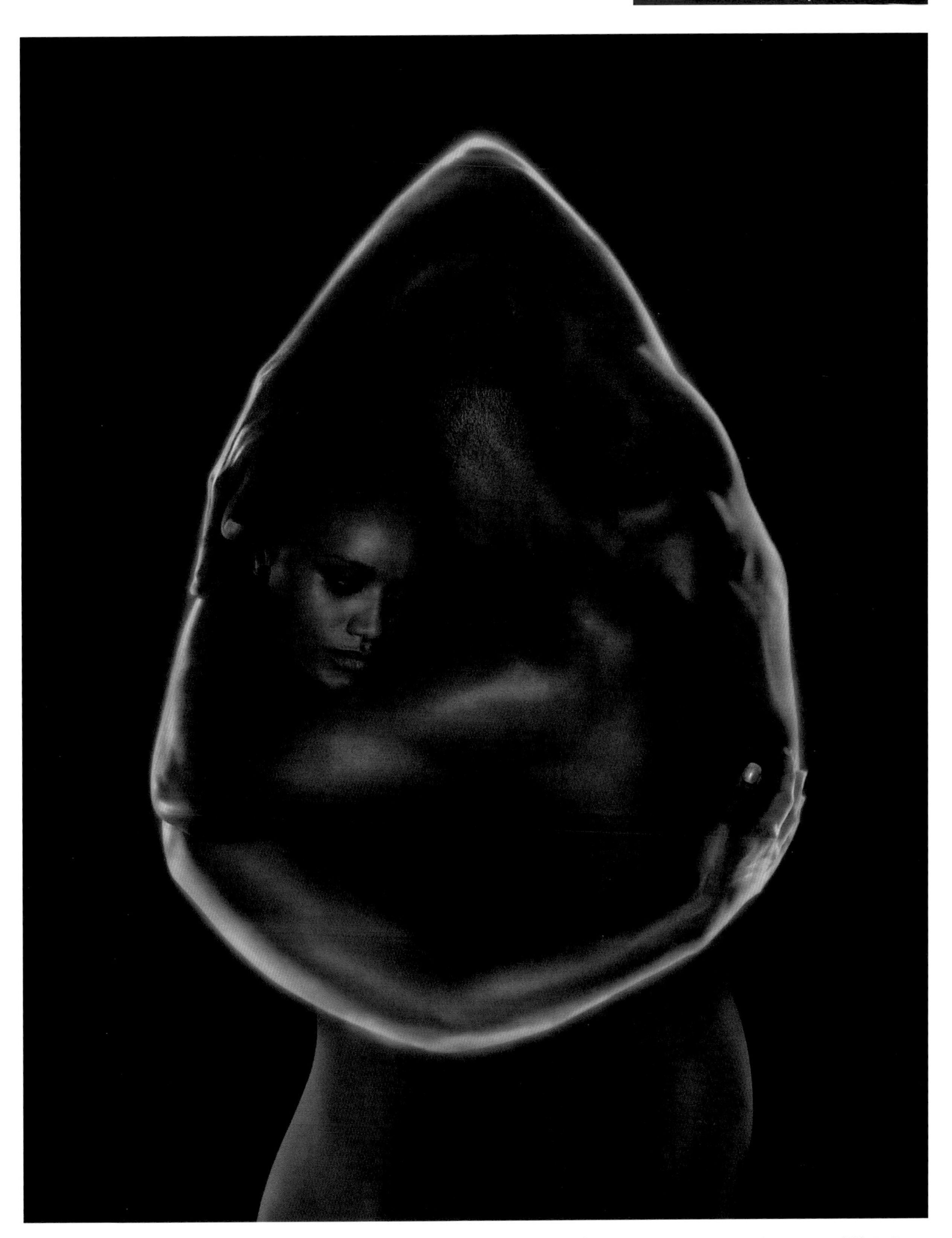

📷: Howard Schatz A: JWT, New York ✏: John Wagner ♛: DeBeers

: Takashi Tsubaki : 8ro art & ad, Tokyo : Suzuki Hachiro : Hanae Mori Open Gallery

: Ricardo Miras : Whispers, Barcelona : Guillermo Fernandez-Huerta : Black Cactus

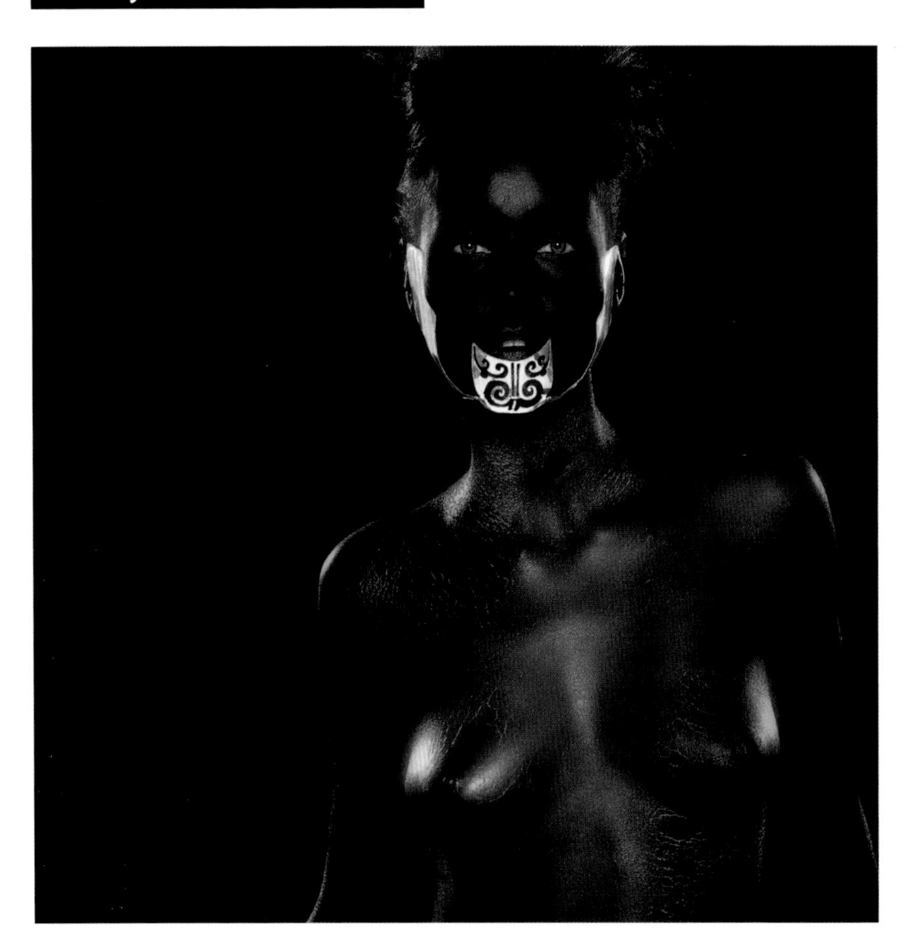

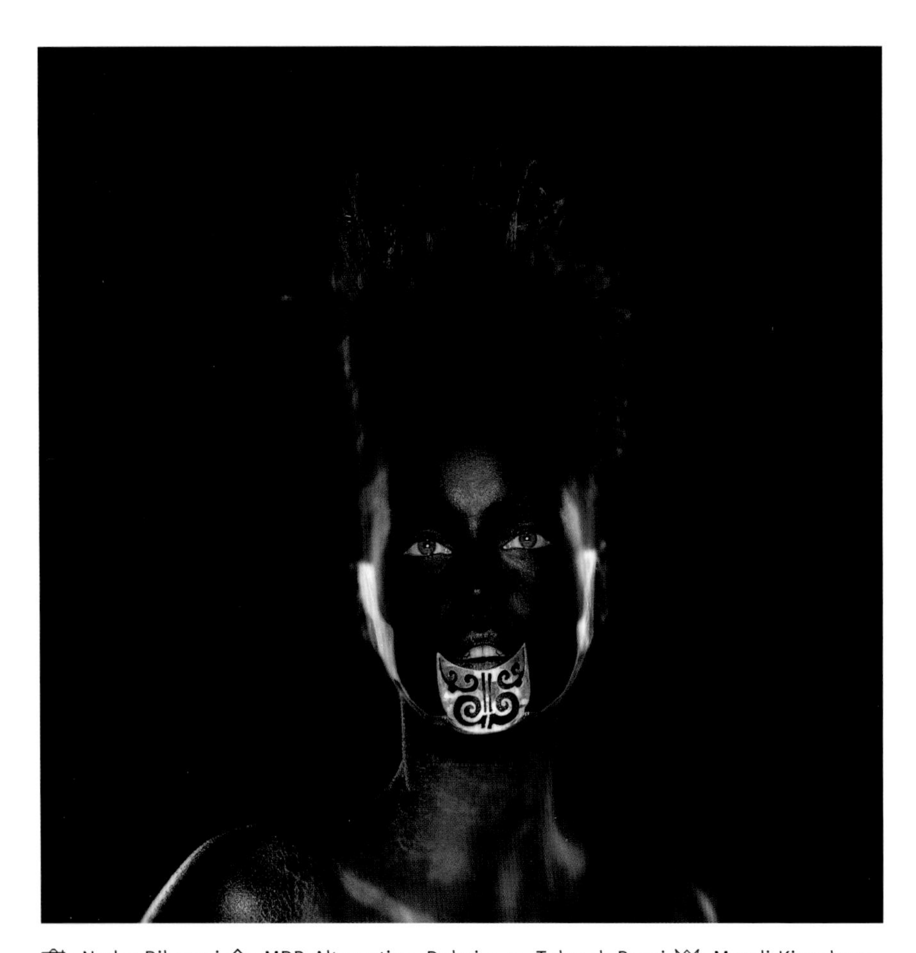

[camera icon]: Nader Bilgrami [agency icon]: MBR Alternative, Dubai [make-up icon]: Tabarak Razvi [model icon]: Mandi Kingsbury

: Fernando Ziviani : Loducca, Curitiba, Brazil : Fábio Miraglia : Abrafoto

: Ricardo Barcellos : Amoroso Studio, São Paulo : Renato Amoroso : FMS

: Erwin Olaf : Armando Testa, Turin : Lantelme Pagani Mendibil : Lavazza

📷: Paolo Pagani ✎: Anna Capettini ♛: Condé Nast

📷: Paolo Pagani ✎: Paola Lombardi ♛: Whitemagazine

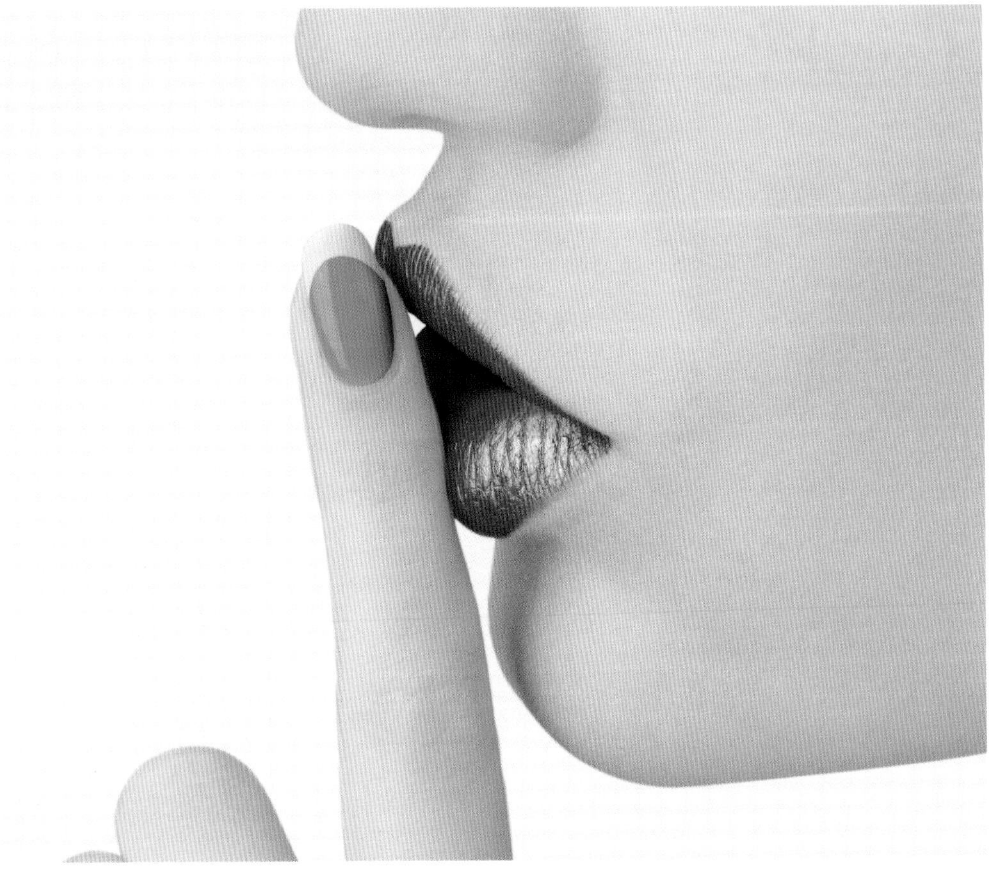

📷: Chris Frazer Smith A: Burkitt DDB, London ✎: Steve Chetham ♛: Peroni

: Sharad Haksar : 1Pointsize, Chennai, India : C.P. Sajith, Payal Shah : Ratika's

: Sharad Haksar : 1Pointsize, Chennai, India : C.P. Sajith : Rachel Hair Stylist

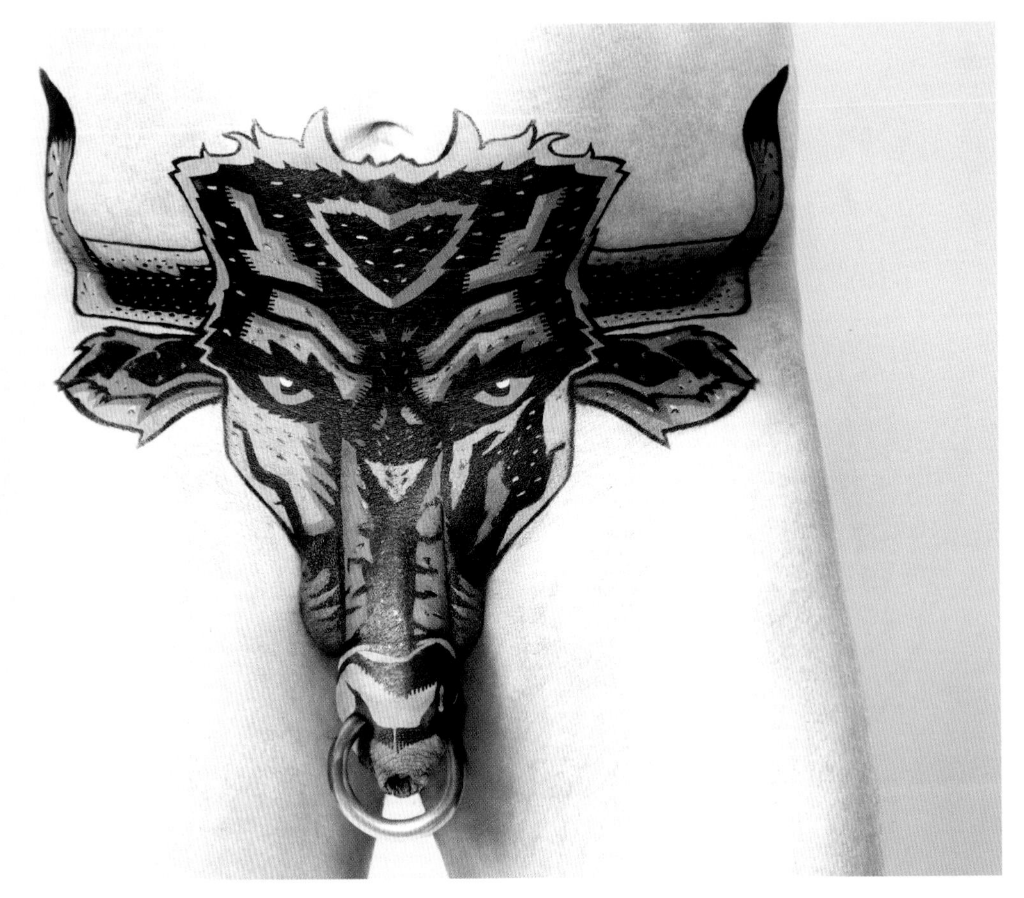

📷: Kurt Stallaert A: Mortierbrigade, Brussels ✎: Koenraad Lefever ♕: Humo

📷: Ramón Serrano A: Delvico Red Cell, Barcelona ✎: Javi Garcia ♕: Asociación Española Contra el Cancer

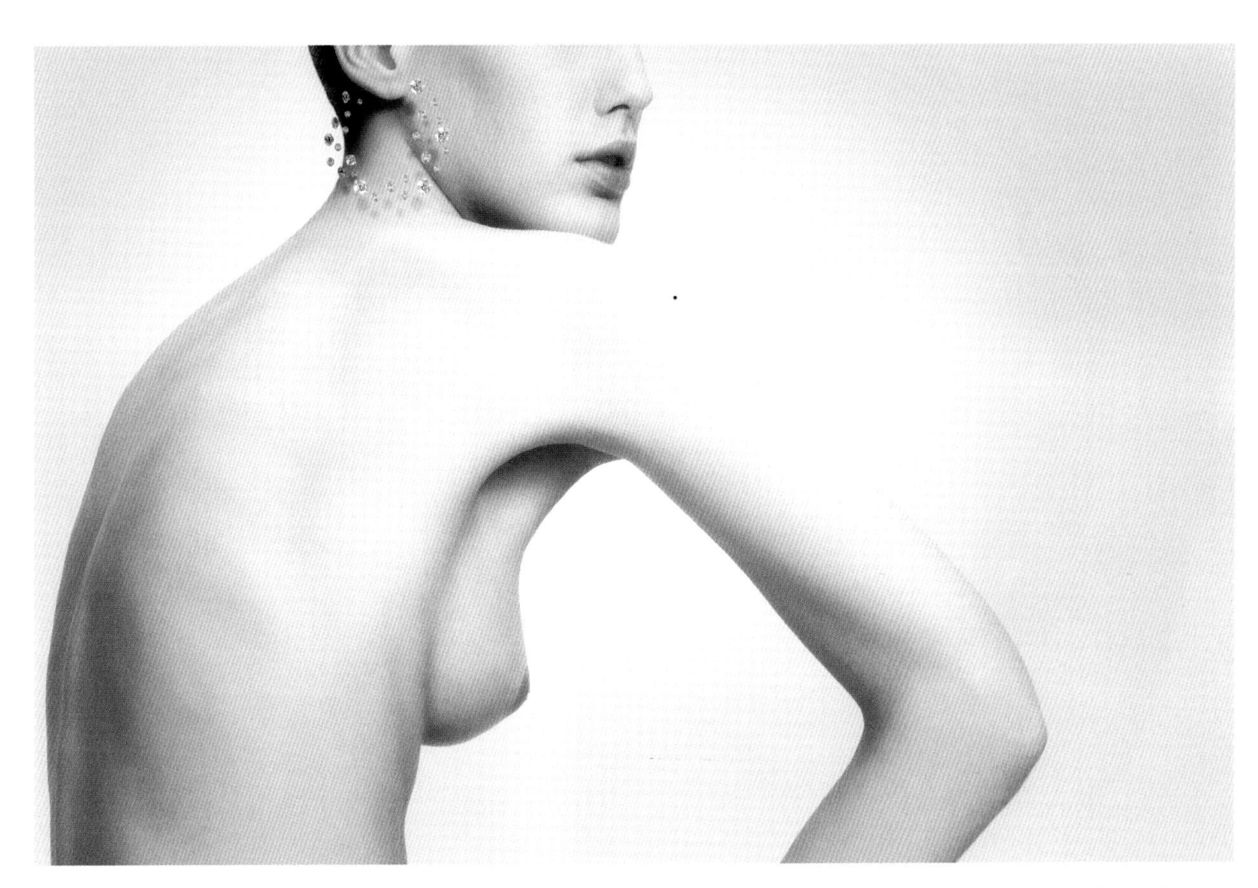

: Kurt Stallaert : Duval Guillaume, Antwerp : Bart Gielen : Dali Jewels

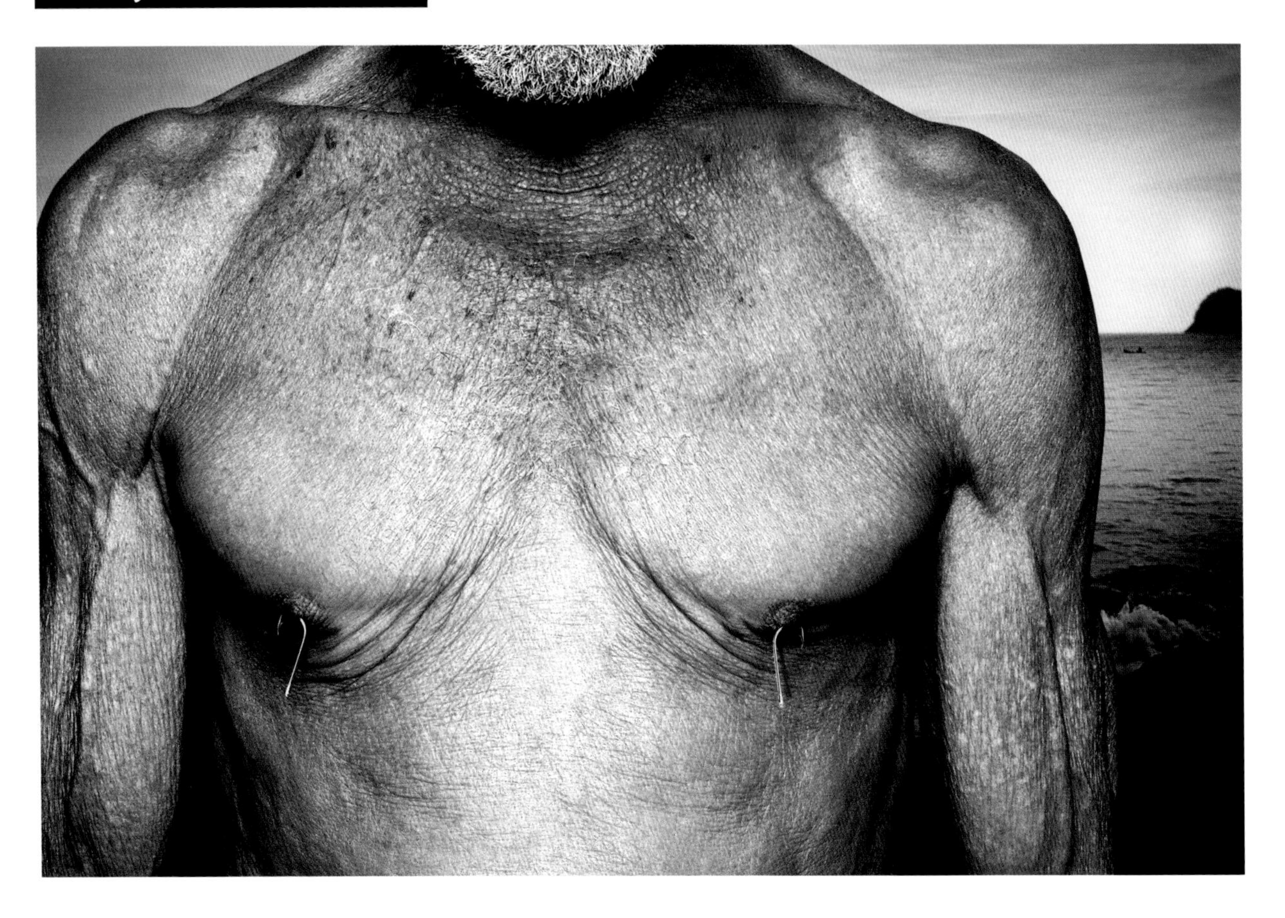

[camera icon]: Rogério Miranda [A icon]: Giovanni FCB, São Paulo [pencil icon]: Renato Lopes, Valdir Bianchi [crown icon]: Pesca Esportiva Magazine

: Ross Brown : Clemenger BBDO, Wellington : Maggie Mouat : Eating Disorder Services

📷: Julien Vonier A: Cavegnwerbung, Zurich ✎: Markus Cavegn ♕: Zürcher Ballett

[camera icon]: Wher Law [A icon]: Hong Kong Trade Development Council Inhouse [pen icon]: Patrick Lam, Natalie Ho [crown icon]: Hong Kong Trade Development Council

: Mark Zibert : Cameron Williamson : Toro Magazine

: Mark Zibert : Carol Moskot : Toronto Life

: Zena Holloway : Young & Rubicam, San Francisco : Ali Mumtaz : Jacuzzi

: Marcel van der Vlugt : Publicis, Amsterdam : Wouter Voges : Renault

📷: Marcel van der Vlugt 👑: Dove

: Daniel Mihail Constantinescu : Daniel Mihail Constantinescu : Printman

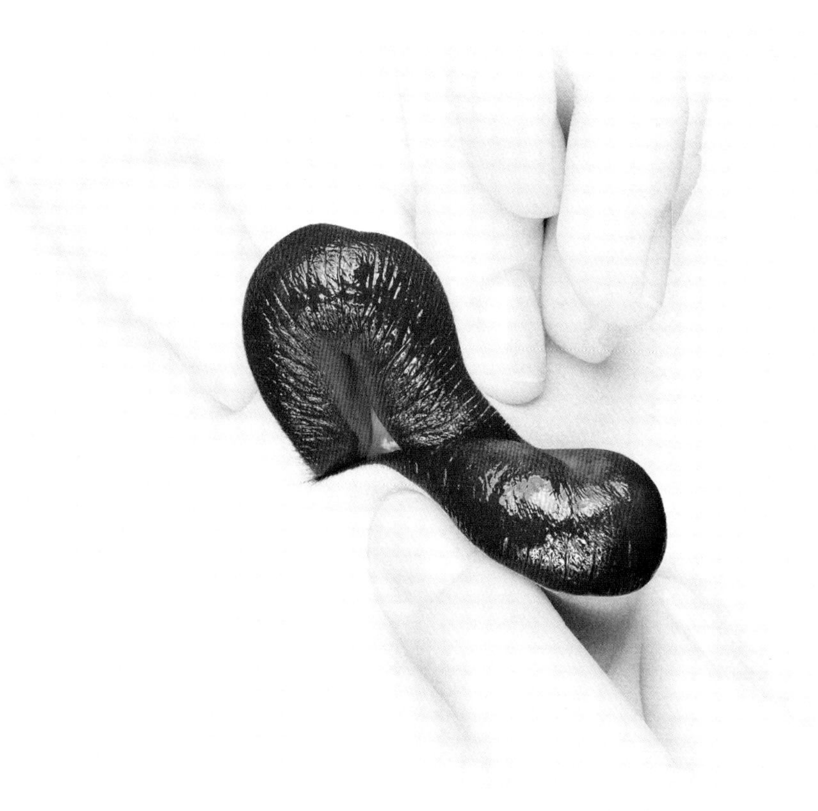

[camera]: Andrea Melcangi [agency]: Beyond the line, Milan [pen]: Joe Butterfeet, Alessandro Borgni [crown]: Martini

📷: Gabi Hirit 👑: Elle

📷: Gerdjan van der Lugt A: Two's Company, Eindhoven, The Netherlands ✎: Dave Carroll ♕: Fasson

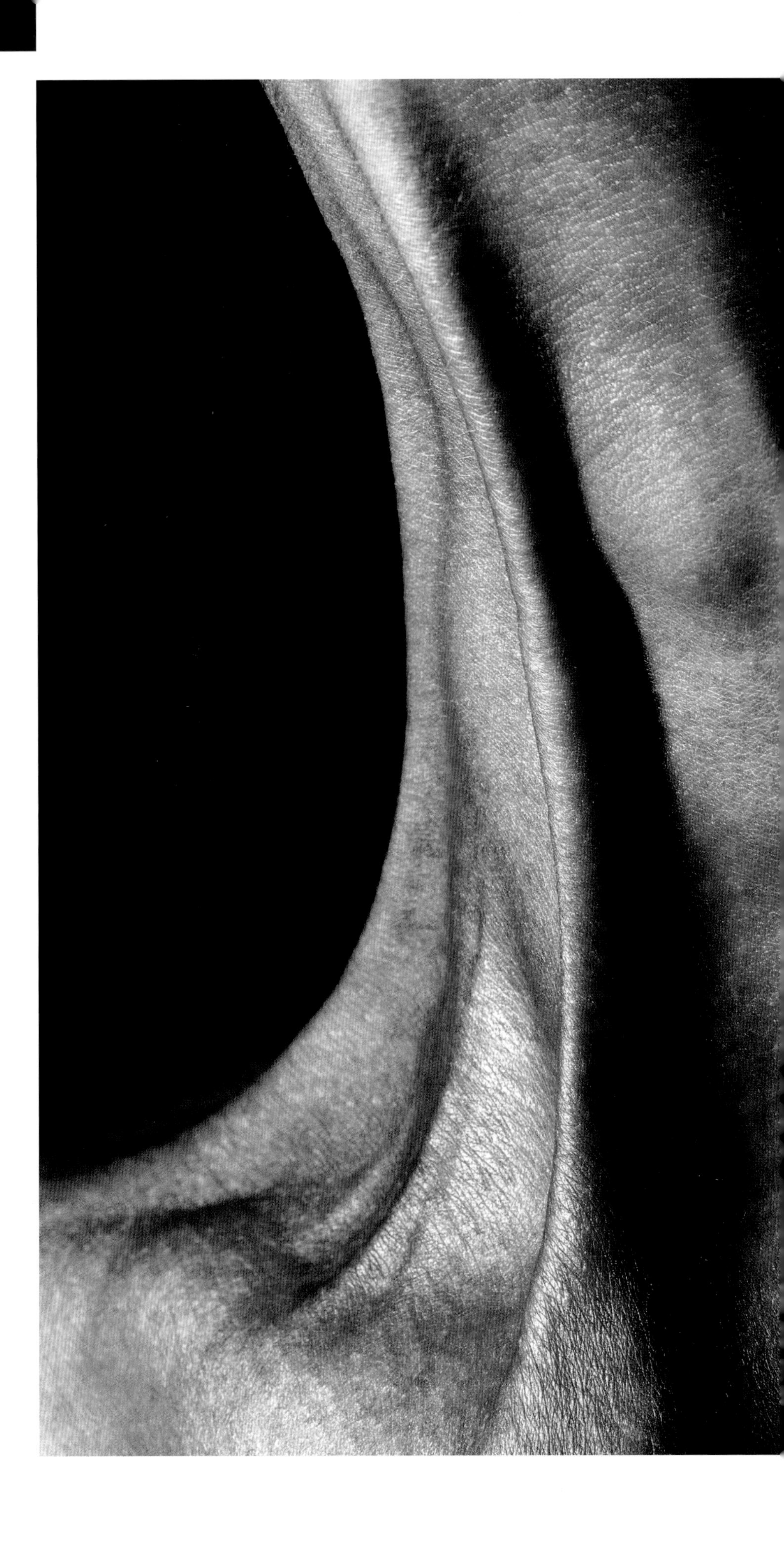

📷: Rafael Costa A: Young & Rubicam, São Paulo ✎: Eugênio Duarte ♔: Greenpeace

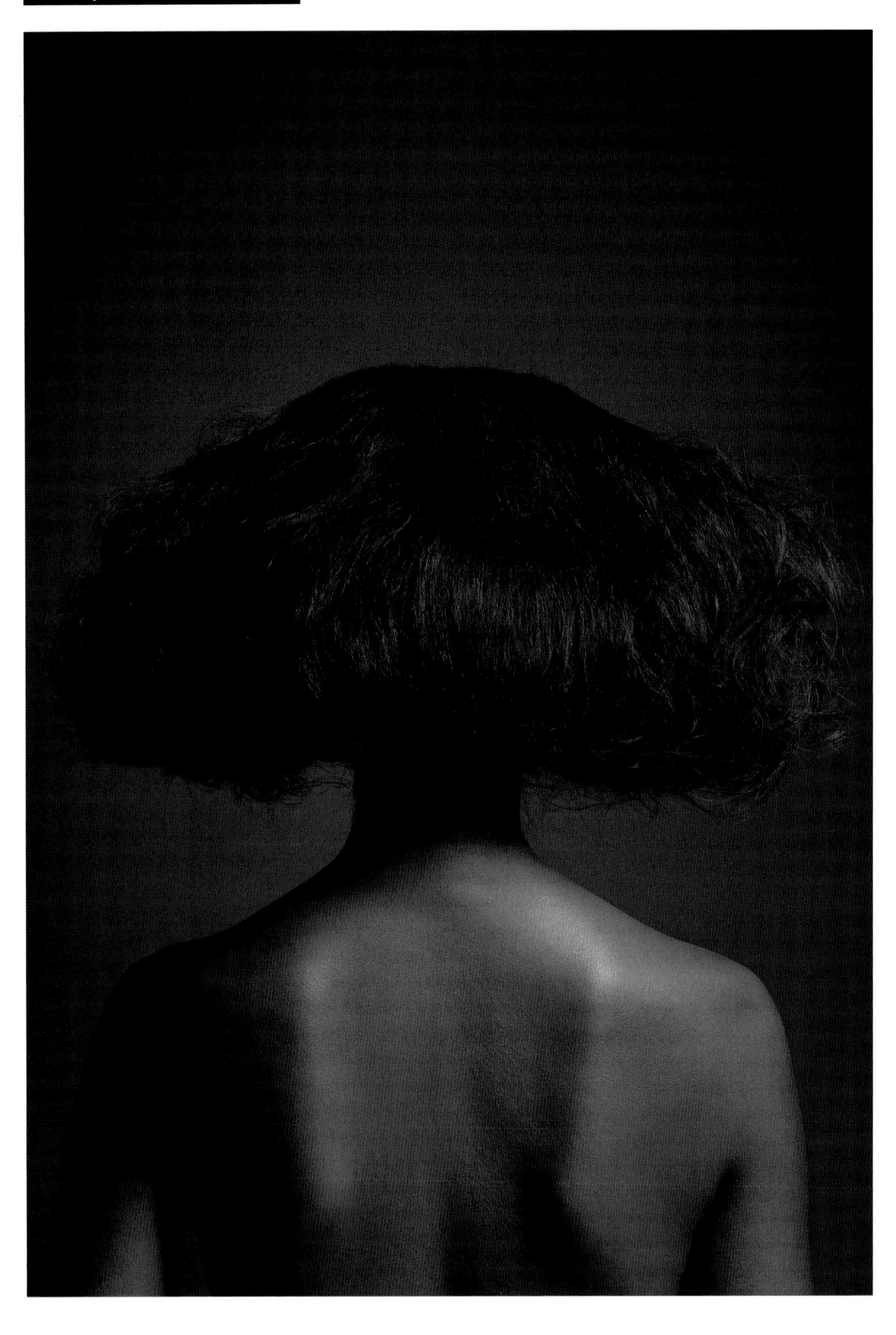

200bph 06.035

📷: Robert Schlatter A: Nordstrom In-house, Seattle ▭: Ursula Brookbank ♛: Nordstrom

📷: Andrzej Dragan A: Scholz & Friends, Warsaw ✏: Piotr Kowalczyk ♛: Hupalo & Wolff

📷: Andrzej Dragan ♛: Foyer Magazine

📷: Kasia Kifert 👑: Maciej Wroblewski/Hair Inspirations

: András Hajdu : Absolut Media, Budapest : Éva Horváth : Haeftling Jailwear

: Shaun Pettigrew : TBWA\Whybin, Auckland : Guy Roberts, Andy Blood : New Zealand Police Recruitment

: Fernando Ziviani : Opus Multipla, Curitiba, Brazil : Cintya Reese : Comunidade Terapêutica Dia

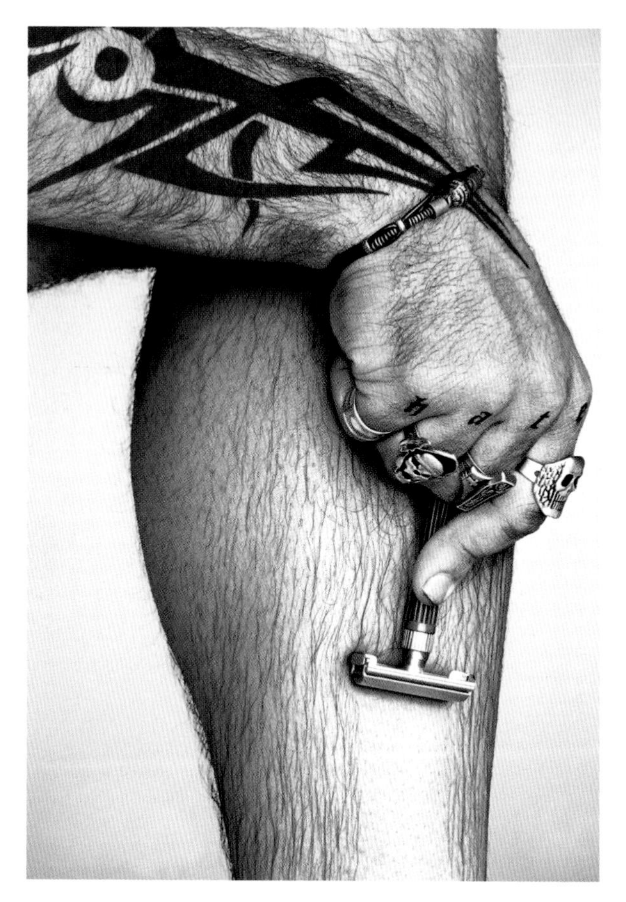

: David Prior : Ogilvy, Johannesburg : Mike Groene-wald : Harley-Davidson

: Garry Simpson : TBWA, Paris : Nick Hine, Jake Rusznyak : BIC

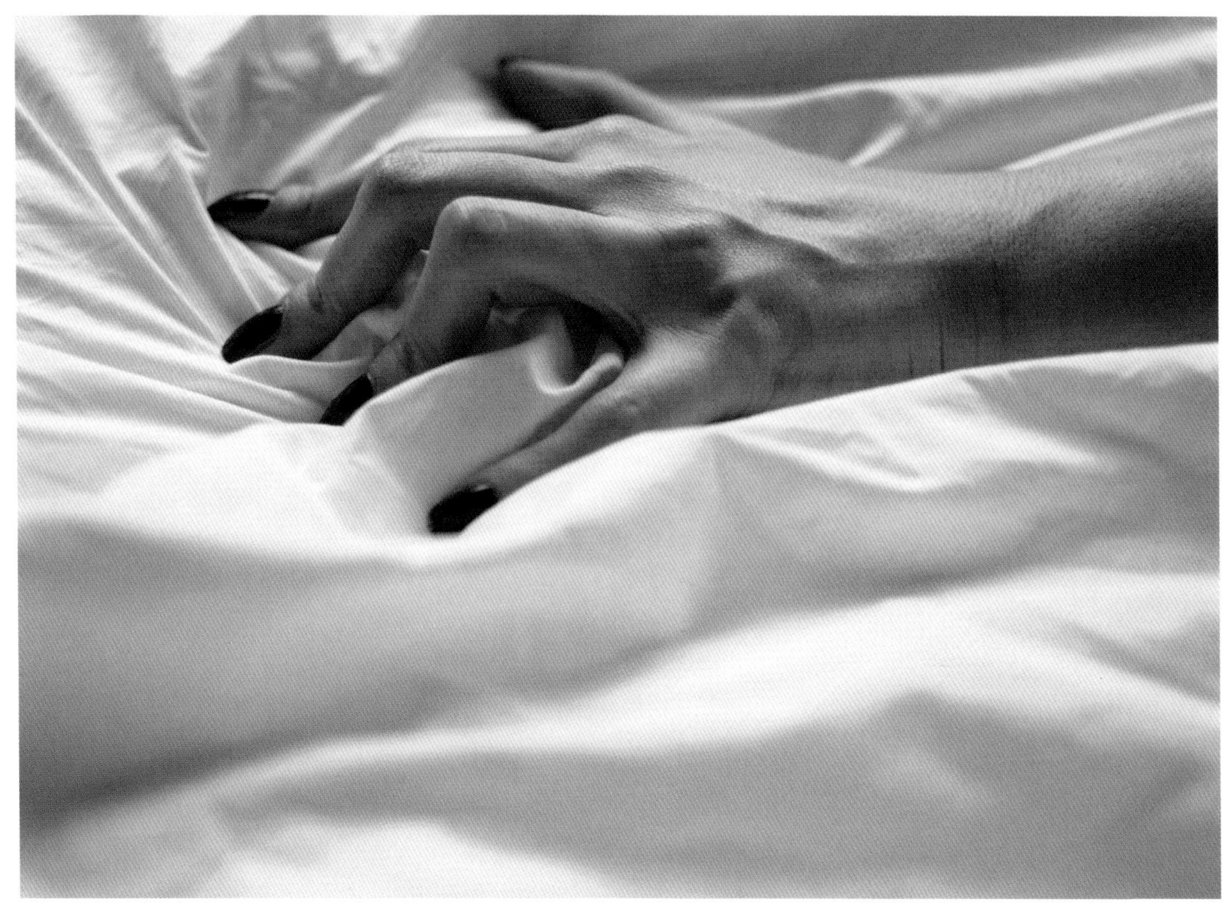

📷: Akira Sakamoto A: Ogilvy & Mather, Tokyo ✎: Keiichi Uemura ♛: Corona

📷: Rodney Schaffer A: Elephant, Melbourne ✎: David Stephens
♕: Kings Pools

📷: Eryk Fitkau A: De Pasquale, Brisbane, Australia ✎: Grant Johnston ♔: Cha Cha Char Wine Bar & Grill

📷: Mark Laita ✎: Pomp Home In-house, San Francisco ✏: Günter Frivert ♕: Pomp Home

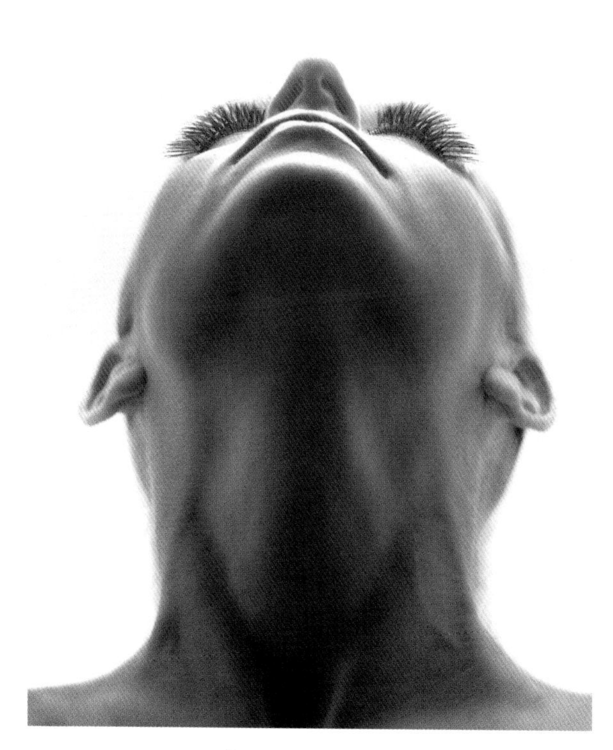

📷: Dennis Manarchy ♕: Radical Media

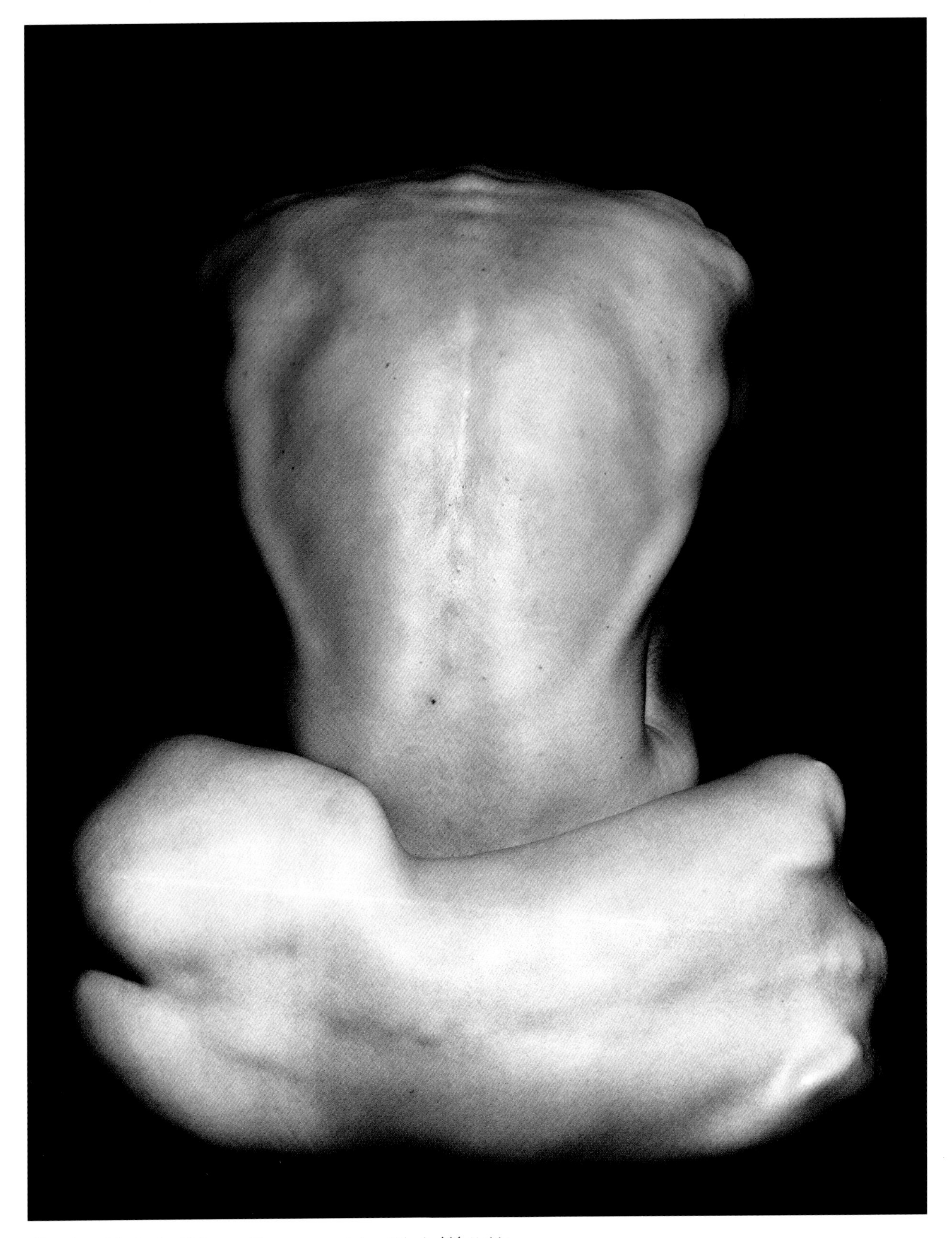

📷: Adam Wlazly A: Alabama, Warsaw ☞: Adam Wlazly ♛: Nokia

📷: Robert Whitman 👑: Self-promotion

📷: Nick Vedros 👑: Canon

: René van der Hulst : Corne Snels : Hardy's Hair Studio

: Jonathan Kantor : Self-promotion

Cover page

: Mike Skelton : The Hunger Project

: James Salzano : Self-promotion

📷: Simon Harsent A: BBDO, New York ✎: Bryan Wilson ♔: M&M's

: Uwe Düttmann : Saatchi & Saatchi, Frankfurt am Main : Anne Petri : FIFA

: Jimmy Fok : Clemenger BBDO, Sydney : Ant Hatton : Legends

📷: Leonardo Vilela A: Publicis, São Paulo ✎: Humberto Fernandez ♔: Telecine

: Martin Sigal : VegaOlmos Ponce, Buenos Aires : Tamara Litovsky : Unilever

📷: Christophe Gilbert A: Duval Guillaume, Brussels ✏: Xavier Bouillon ♛: ANGCP

📷: Will van Overbeek A: Element 79 Partners, Chicago ✎: David Boensch ♔: Quaker Oats

: Florian Geiss : Lowe, Zurich : David Dudler : Orange

📷: Stuart Crossett A: Leo Burnett, Melbourne ✎: Tone Walde, Craig Jackson ♔: Anglicare Victoria

📷: Uwe Düttmann A: M.E.C.H., Berlin ✎: Thorsten Adenauer ♔: Lufthansa

📷: Tony D'Orio A: Blackwerk, Chicago ▭: Eric Stein, Kathy Petrauskas ♕: Chicago Canine Rescue

📷: Chris Frazer Smith A: Australie, Paris ▭: Frédéric Royer ♕: l'Enfant Bleu

[camera]: Frank Herholdt [A]: Getty Images In-house, London [pencil]: Emma Sutton [crown]: Getty Images

📷: Wendelien Daan 👑: Self-promotion

📷: Heimo Schmidt ✎: Kara Wetherby ♕: Spaksmannspjarir

: David Allan Brandt : Lowe & Partners/Live, Hong Kong : Kinson Chan, Tim Yung : Tough Jeans

📷: Mads Lauritzen A: Co+Høgh, Copenhagen ▭: Claus Møllebro ♕: REDGREEN

📷: James Day A: DDB, London ✎: Justin Tindall ♛: Harvey Nichols

📷: Geof Kern A: Douglas Joseph Partners, Los Angeles ✎: Doug Joseph ♛: Vent-A-Hood

📷: Geof Kern ⌂: Neiman Marcus In-house, Dallas ✎: Tony Balquin ♔: Neiman Marcus

📷: Stewart Cohen ✎: Chuck Harris ♔: Visual Arts Group

: Paolo Pagani : Anna Capettini : Condé Nast

: Kousaku Hirano : Hiroki Kusui : Ei Shuppansha

📷: Kazunali Tajima 👑: Eater

📷: Vincent Dixon A: Publicis Conseil, Paris ▭: Frédéric Royer ♕: Wonderbra

📷: Stewart Cohen A: FFWD, Dallas ✏: Scott LeBlanc ♕: Hollywood Casino

: YangTan : BaseNYC, New York : Dimitri Jeurissen : Tribeca Grand Hotel

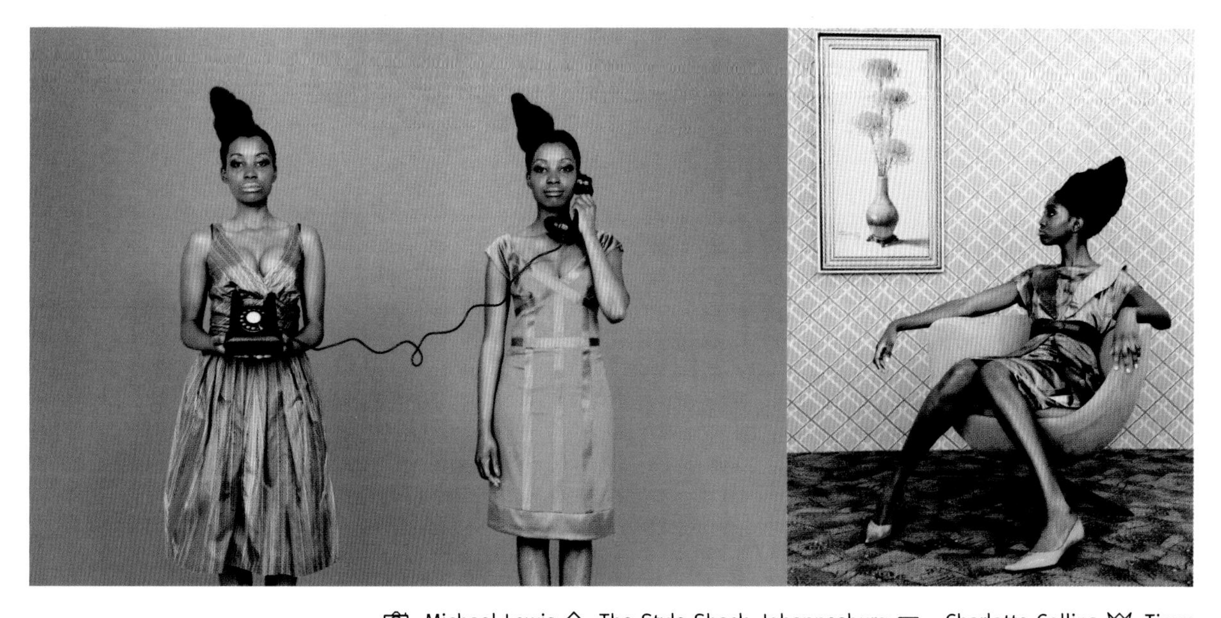

: Michael Lewis : The Style Shack, Johannesburg : Charlotte Collins : Timm

: Lewis Ho : Leo Burnett, Hong Kong : Man To Yiu : One2Free

[camera icon]: Takeshi Hanzawa [pen icon]: Takeshi Hanzawa [crown icon]: Super

📷: Winkler & Noah A: Lapiu, Rome ✂: Giambattista Menna 👑: Music Box

: Nick & Chloé : Levi's In-house, Paris : Nick & Chloé : Levi's Kids

📷: David Emmite A: Nike In-house, Beaverton, Oregon ✎: Mike Dawson ♛: Nike

📷: Connie Hong ✎: Peter Kwok ♔: P.M.C. Jewelry

📷: Connie Hong A: Leo Burnett, Hong Kong ✎: Gordon Hughes ♔: BenQ-Siemens

: Antonio Barrella : B› Magazine ADV, Milan : Valentina Ilardi, Emiliano Marchionni : B› Magazine

: Antonio Barrella : Studio Orizzonte, Rome : Valentina Ilardi : B› Magazine

📷: Antonio Barrella A: Studio Orizzonte, Rome ✏: Valentina Ilardi, Antonio Barrella ♕: Istituto Europeo di Design

📷: Jefunne Gimpel ✏: Jefunne Gimpel 👑: Future Image

: Joan Garrigosa : Ruiz Nicoli Líneas, Madrid : Cesar Lopez : Cardhu

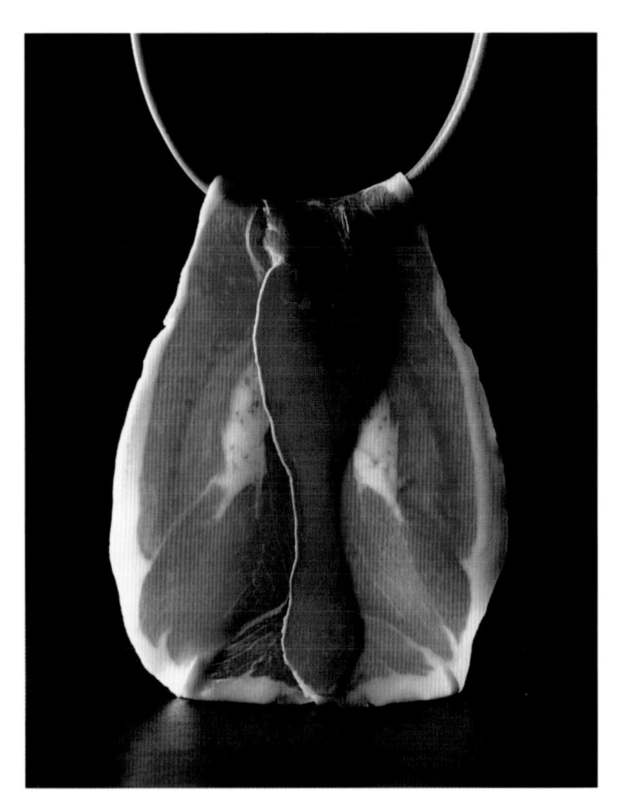

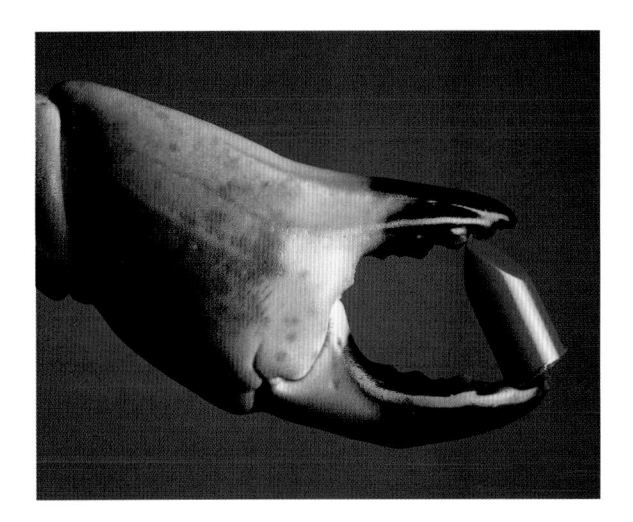

: Patrice De Villiers : Selfridges In-house, Leicester, United Kingdom : Patrice de Villiers : Selfridges

📷: Jaap Stahlie A: Quote Media, Amsterdam ▭: Jannie van de Goor ♛: Safe Magazine

📷: Tommy Naess A: Boska Reklame, Bergen, Norway ✎: Øyvind Boska ♛: WahWah Skin Trim Studio

: Uwe Düttmann : Publicis, New York : Alex Lea : Amstel

: Hajime Watanabe : JWT Japan, Tokyo : Asako Oshima : Häagen-Dazs

: Hajime Watanabe : SUN-AD, Tokyo : Junichi Kojima : Suntory

: Anuchai Secharunputong : Creative Juice/G1, Bangkok : Thirasak Tanapatanakul, Kittitat Larppitakpong : Tamiya

📷: Rainer Stratmann A: Hahnemühle In-house, Dassel, Germany ✎: Rainer Stratmann ♛: Hahnemühle

📷: Rainer Stratmann A: Team One, Los Angeles ✎: James Hendry ♛: Lexus

[camera icon]: Alex Telfer [agency icon]: Good Creative, Glasgow [client icon]: Bunnahabhain

📷: Christian Schmidt A: Ogilvy & Mather, New York ✎: Jim Larmon ♔: Delta Airlines

📷: Christian Schmidt A: Loeffler Ketchum Mountjoy, Charlotte, North Carolina ✎: Doug Pederson ♔: North Carolina Tourism

📷: Christian Schmidt A: Ogilvy & Mather, New York ✎: Damien Eley ♔: American Express

📷: Christian Schmidt A: Young & Rubicam, Irvine, California ✎: Tricia Ting ♔: Jaguar

📷: Michael Schnabel 👑: Self-promotion

Photographer: Erik Almås Agency: RR Partners, Arizona Art Director: Richard Haynie, Kevin Munk Client: Blue Cross Blue Shield

📷: Alex Telfer A: The Chase, Manchester 👑: Yorkshire Water

📷: Alex Telfer A: Different, Newcastle, United Kingdom ✎: Simon Storey 👑: One North East

: Simon Stock : Team One, Los Angeles : Julia Hasbrook : Lexus

: Smári : Arnold Worldwide, Boston : Brandon Sides : Timberland

[camera icon]: Michael Schnabel [agency icon]: DDB, London [contact icon]: Karen Hagemann [client icon]: Neutrogena

[camera icon]: Michael Schnabel [agency icon]: RTS Rieger Team, Stuttgart, Germany [contact icon]: Boris Pollig [client icon]: Baustahlgewebe

Smári : Young & Rubicam, Irvine, California : Tricia Ting : Orange County Pacific Symphony

: Steve Bronstein : Lowe, Mexico City : Miguel Angel Bolio : Camel

📷: Richard Hamilton Smith A: Periscope, Minneapolis ✎: Brien Spanier, Patrick Weld ♔: Arctic Cat

: Winkler & Noah : Self-promotion

: Steve Bonini : Carmichael Lynch, Minneapolis : Ray Fesenmaier : Harley-Davidson

📷: Chris von Menge A: Publicis Mojo, Melbourne ✎: David Klein ♔: Nike

📷: Stuart Hall A: Dunkin Design, West Midlands, United Kingdom ▭: Stuart Hall
♕: Rushton Real Estate

📷: William Huber A: Team One, Los Angeles ✎: Kevin Mitchell ♕: Lexus

📷: William Huber A: Outside Magazine In-house, Santa Fe, New Mexico ✎: Rob Haggart ♕: Outside Magazine

📷: William Huber ⌂: Team One, Los Angeles ✎: Kevin Mitchell ♕: Lexus

📷: Chai Guan Teo 👑: Self-promotion

📷: Darran Rees A: Host Universal, London ✐: Robin Smith ♛: Cafedirect

📷: Andy Glass A: Lowe, London ✐: Eliot Wykes ♛: Coca-Cola

📷: Kousaku Hirano ✎: Hiroki Kusui ♛: Ei Shuppansha

📷: Ramón Serrano ⌂: DDB, Barcelona ✎: Xavier Solé ♔: Audi

📷: Marcelo Coelho A: Tom, Belo Horizonte, Brazil ✎: Vinicius Alzamora ♕: State Government of Minas Gerais

: Peter Leverman : Target, St. John's, Newfoundland : Tom Murphy : Newfoundland Tourism

: Peter Leverman : SGCI, Sackville, Canada : Neil McCulloch : Stanfield's

: Peter Leverman : Northlich, Cincinnati, Ohio : Eric Thompson : Humana

: Peter Leverman : SGCI, Sackville, Canada : Neil McCulloch : Stanfield's

📷: Peter Leverman A: Target, St. John's, Newfoundland ✎: Tom Murphy ♕: Newfoundland Tourism

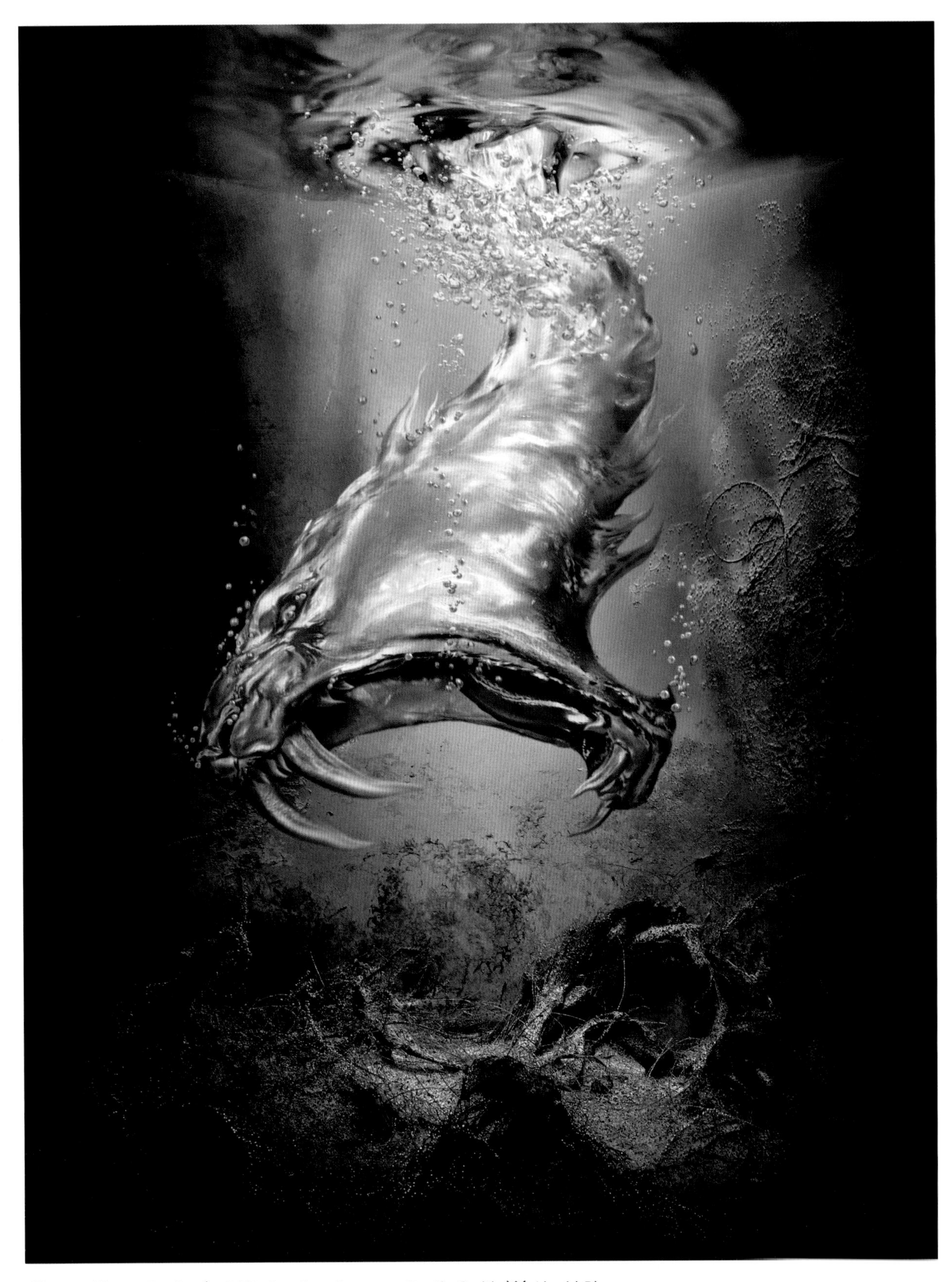

📷: Staudinger+Franke A: DDB, San Francisco ✏: Dustin Smith ♕: Liquid-Plumr

[camera]: Mike Skelton [pen]: Mike Skelton [crown]: The Hunger Project

📷: Michael Eastman ♔: Self-promotion

📷: Tim Simmons 👑: Self-promotion

📷: Philip Rostron A: MacLaren McCann, Toronto ✎: Rich Buceta ♕: General Motors

📷: Antti Viitala 👑: Stockmann

📷: Jan Willem Scholten A: GBK Heye, Munich ✎: Zelko Pezely 👑: Süddeutsche Zeitung

📷: Winkler & Noah 🏆: Self-promotion

📷: Ari Magg ⌂: Jónsson & Lemacks, Reykjavík ✎: Viggo Jónsson ♔: Reyka Vodka

📷: Christopher Thomas A: Network!, Munich 👑: Schirmer/Mosel

: Jørgen Reimer : McBride, Stockholm : Lena McBride : Woolpower

📷: Chai Guan Teo 🖂: Self-promotion

📷: Vikas Dutt 🖂: Adroit Solutions

📷: David Allan Brandt A: Team/Young & Rubicam, Dubai ✎: Komal Bedi, Sam Ahmed ♛: Emaar

📷: Klaus Mitteldorf 👑: Self-promotion

📷: Klaus Mitteldorf 👑: Self-promotion

📷: Klaus Mitteldorf 👑: Vogue

📷: Klaus Mitteldorf 👑: Elle

[camera icon]: Bernard Bertrand [agency icon]: DDB, Brussels [pen icon]: Sebastian Piacentini [crown icon]: White Night

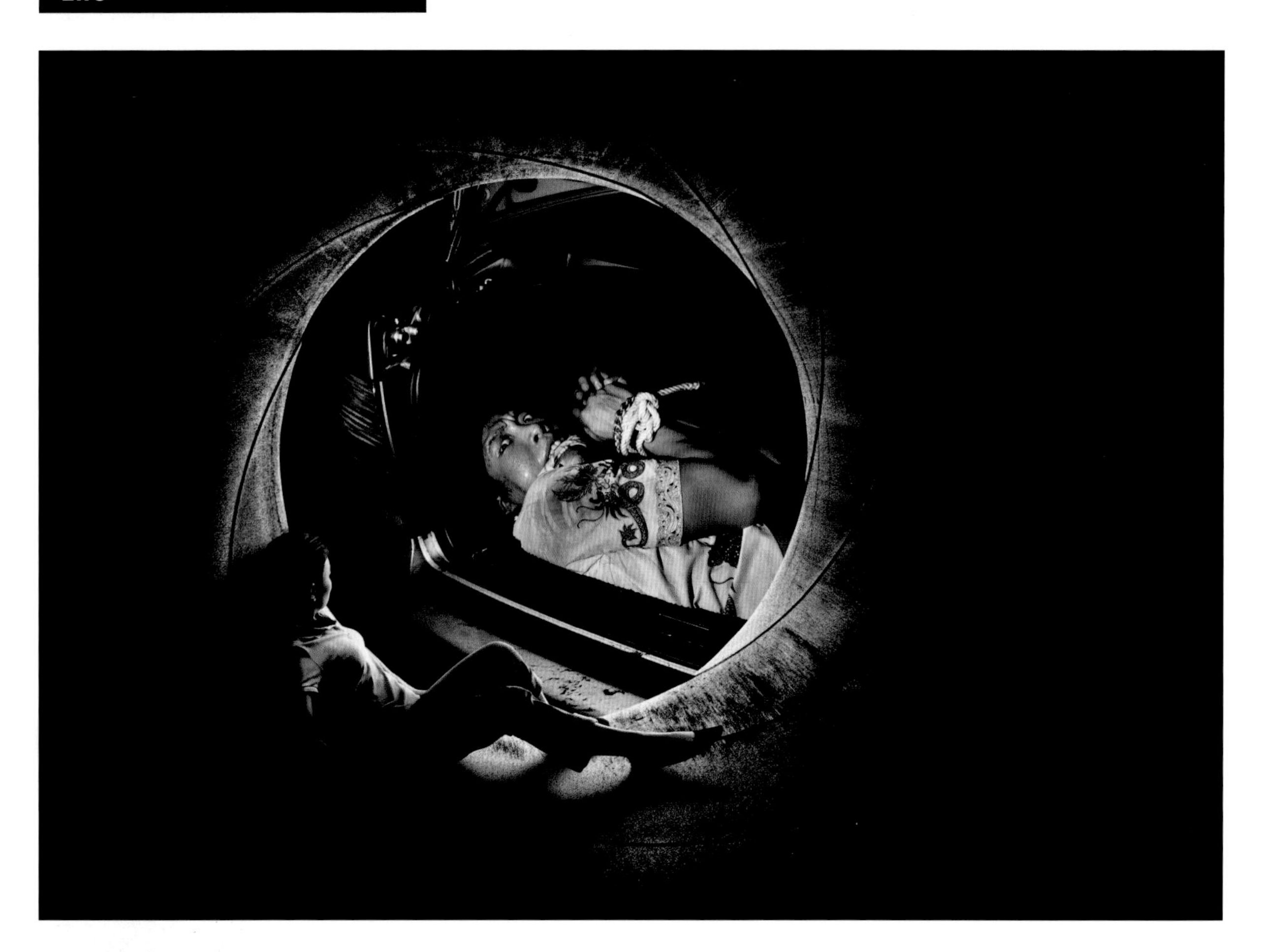

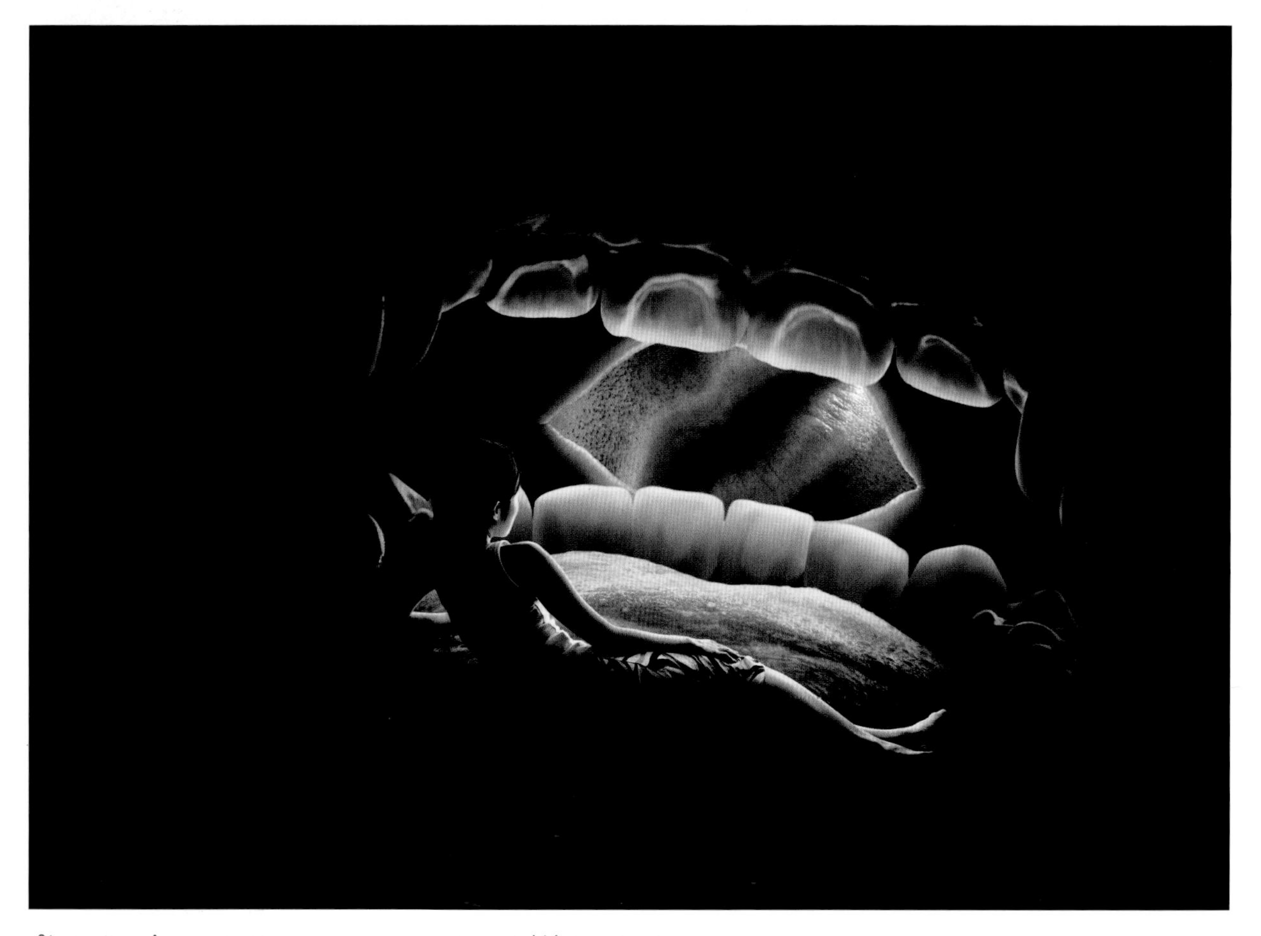

📷: Szeling A: BBDO, Singapore ✎: Wee Kim Goh ♕: Acmabooks.com

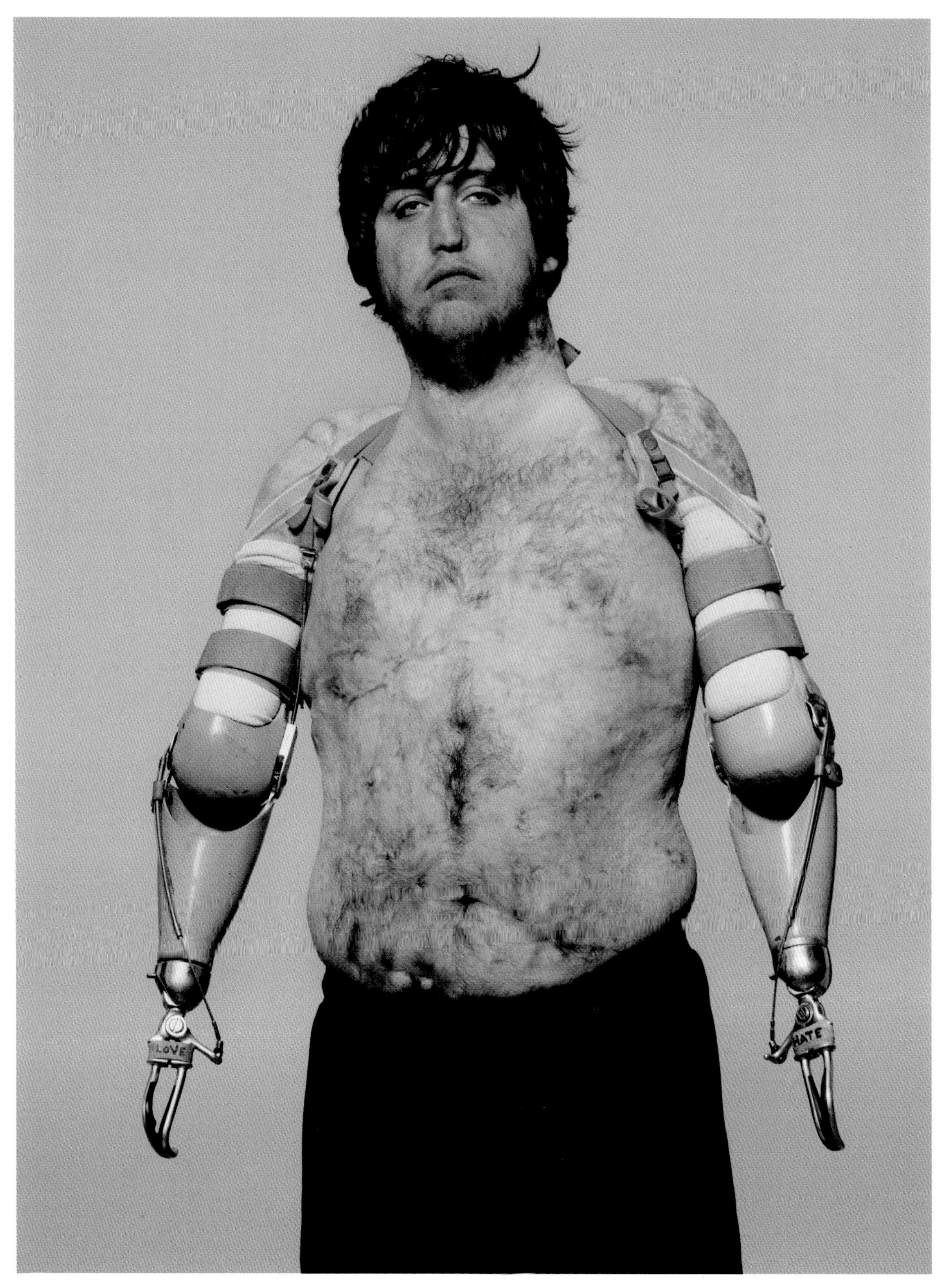

📷: Andreas Smetana A: Cassius Clay, Sydney ▭: Michael Spirkovski ♕: WorkCover New South Wales

: Ricardo Cunha : Giovanni FCB, Rio de Janeiro : Carlos André Eyer : Vizoo Magazine

: Tony D'Orio : Leo Burnett, Chicago : Noel Haan, Adrien Bindi : Altoids

📷: Aernout Overbeeke A: BBDO Campaign, Stuttgart, Germany ✎: Armin Jochum ♔: Kamitei Foundation

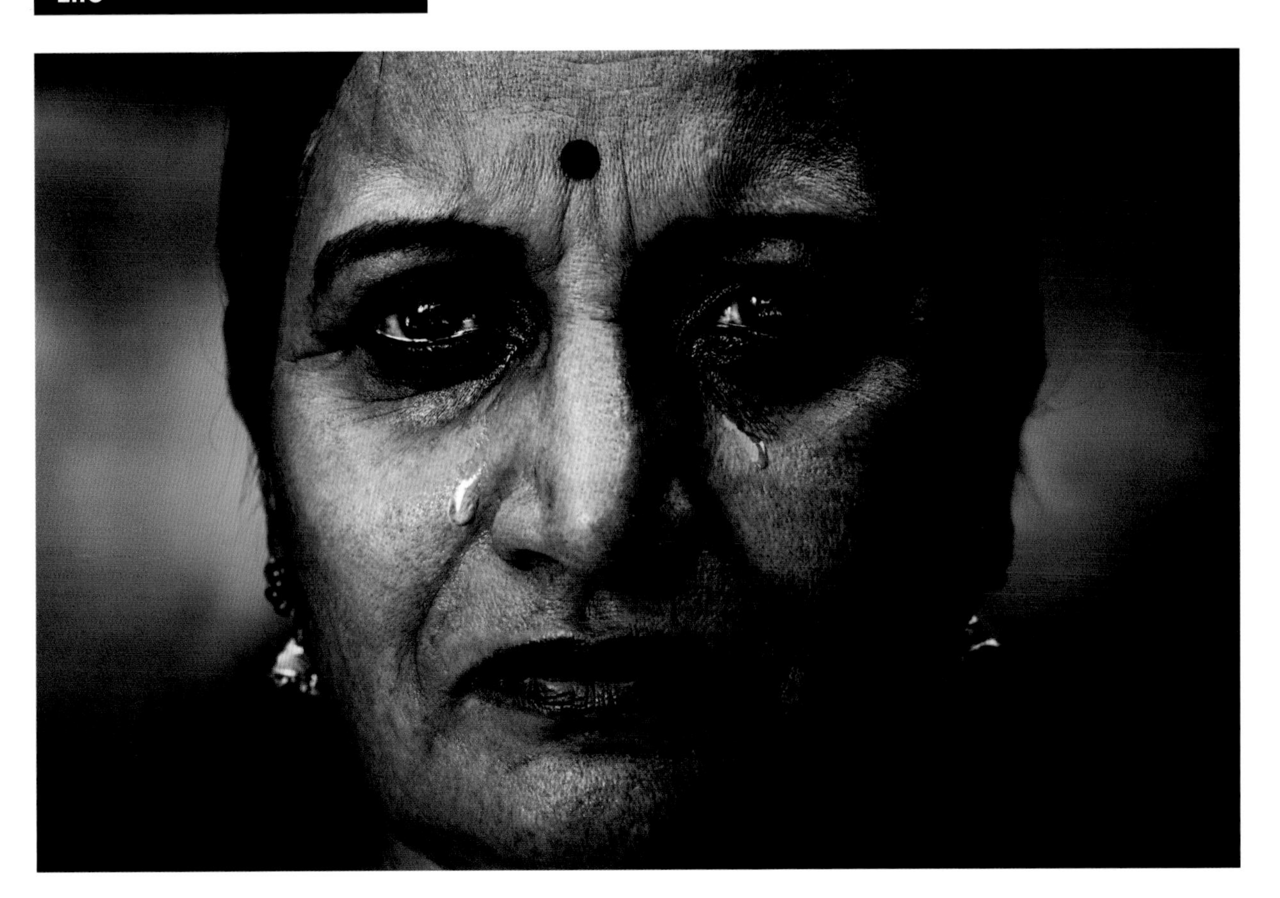

: Manolo Moran : F/Nazca Saatchi & Saatchi, São Paulo : Bruno Prosperi : FS Casting

📷: Marcia Ramalho A: AlmapBBDO, São Paulo ✍: Renato Fernandez, Roberto Fernandez 👑: Radio Bandeirantes

📷: Norbert Kniat A: Malkasten, Vienna ✍: Roman Keller 👑: Active Beauty Magazine

: Rainer Stratmann : In Medias Rees, Stuttgart, Germany : Simone Rees : Knauf Insulation

: Rainer Stratmann : Köckritzdörrich, Reutlingen, Germany : Lutz Sündermann : Lamborghini

📷: Rainer Stratmann A: In Medias Rees, Stuttgart, Germany ✎: Simone Rees ♛: Knauf Insulation

: Seth Taras H: Ground Zero, Los Angeles : Jeff Lablo : The History Channel

: Blinkk : TBWA, London : Graham Cappi : Eurostar

: Blinkk : Fabris Lane In-house, Surrey, United Kingdom : Sammy Farrington : Fabris Lane

: Steve Bonini : 40/40, Berkeley, California : John Trotter : Keen Footwear

: Szeling : Leo Burnett, Singapore : Jon Loke : Singapore Press Holdings

: Stuart Crossett : Grey Worldwide, Melbourne : Tim Holmes : Open Family

📷: Nick Meek ⍝: McCann Erickson, London ✎: Mark Reddy ♕: American Airlines

📷: Sean Izzard A: Saatchi & Saatchi, Sydney ✎: Andy Dilallo, Jay Benjamin ♛: Olympus

📷: Jonathan Tay A: Bates Asia, Singapore ✎: Minzie Liyu ♔: Nokia

📷: Edo Kars ⌂: Locomotive, Amsterdam ✎: Kees Rijken ♛: Athlon

📷: Pierpaolo Ferrari A: Red Cell, Milan ✎: Federico Pepe ♕: Alfa Romeo

📷: Pierpaolo Ferrari ✎: Paola Manfrin ♕: Le Dictateur

: Ljubodrag Andric : Self-promotion

: James Salzano : Cline, Davis & Mann, New York : Ralph Skorge : Pfizer

📷: Michael Blann A: Getty Images In-house, London ✎: Michael Blann ♕: Getty Images

📷: Jaap Stahlie A: SO Design, Amsterdam ✎: Jan Sevenster ♕: NIBC Wealth Management

: Goran Tacevski : Leo Burnett, Prague : Jiri Langpaul : Kafka Museum

📷: Alan McFetridge A: Saatchi & Saatchi, Singapore ✏: Colin Jeffery ♛: Lexus

: Stefano Gilera : Lowe Pirella, Milan : Alessandra Paglialonga : La Repubblica

📷: Andy Glass A: TBWA, Paris ▭: Sophie Guyon ♛: Absolut Vodka

: Magda Wunsche : Parliament Cigarettes In-house, Warsaw : Parliament Cigarettes

: Marc Gouby : Publicis Conseil, Paris : Jorge Carreno : Renault

📷: Uwe Düttmann A: M.E.C.H., Berlin ✏: Thorsten Adenauer ♔: Lufthansa

📷: Vincent Dixon A: Publicis Conseil, Paris ✏: Frédéric Royer ♔: Wonderbra

: Vincent Dixon : Strawberry Frog, Amsterdam : Jason Schragger : Heineken

: Vincent Dixon : TBWA\Chiat\Day, Los Angeles : Tom Gibson : PlayStation 2

[camera icon]: Jean-Yves Lemoigne [A icon]: Publicis Conseil, Paris [pen icon]: Charles Guillemant [crown icon]: Sagem

: Jean-Yves Lemoigne : DDB, Paris : Pierrette Diaz : Volkswagen

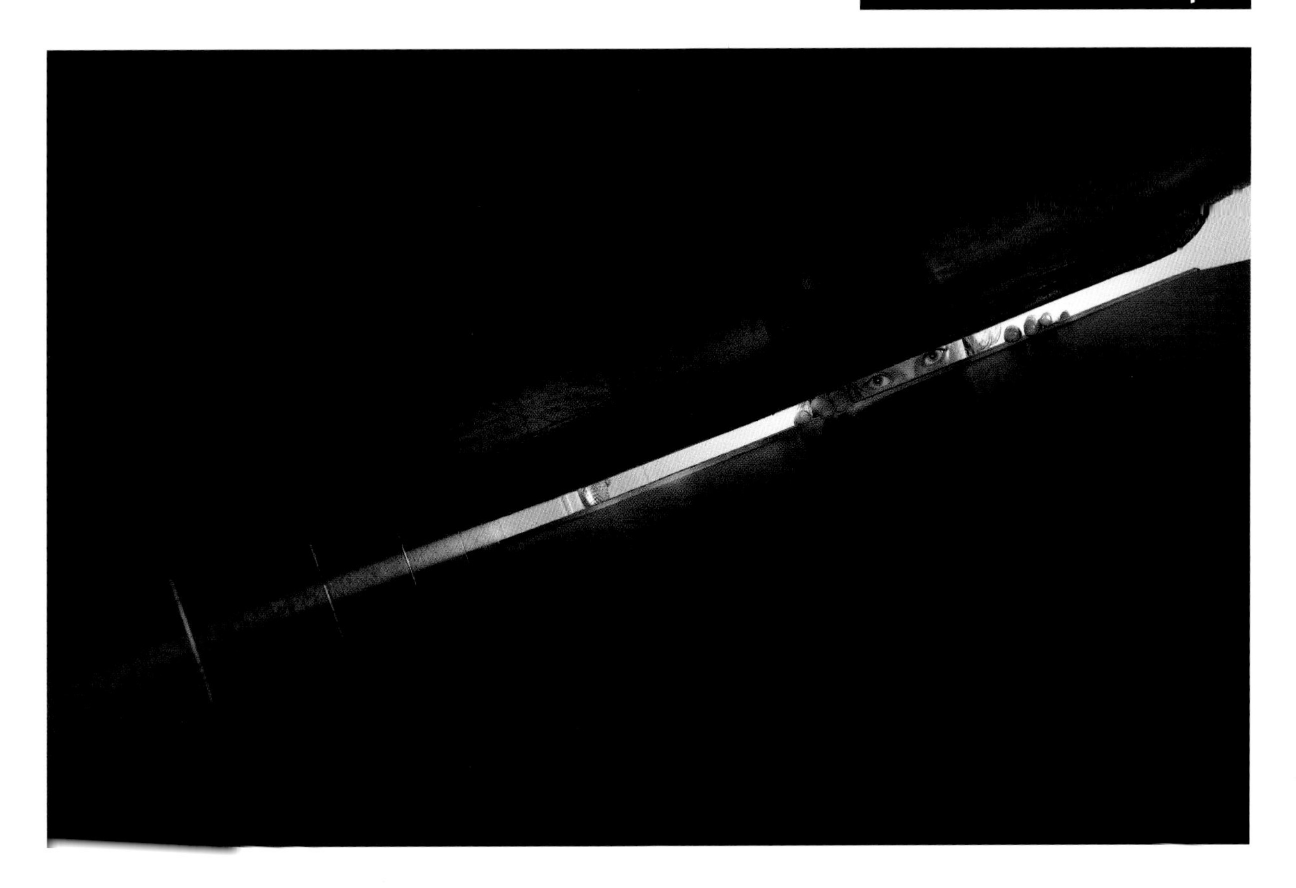

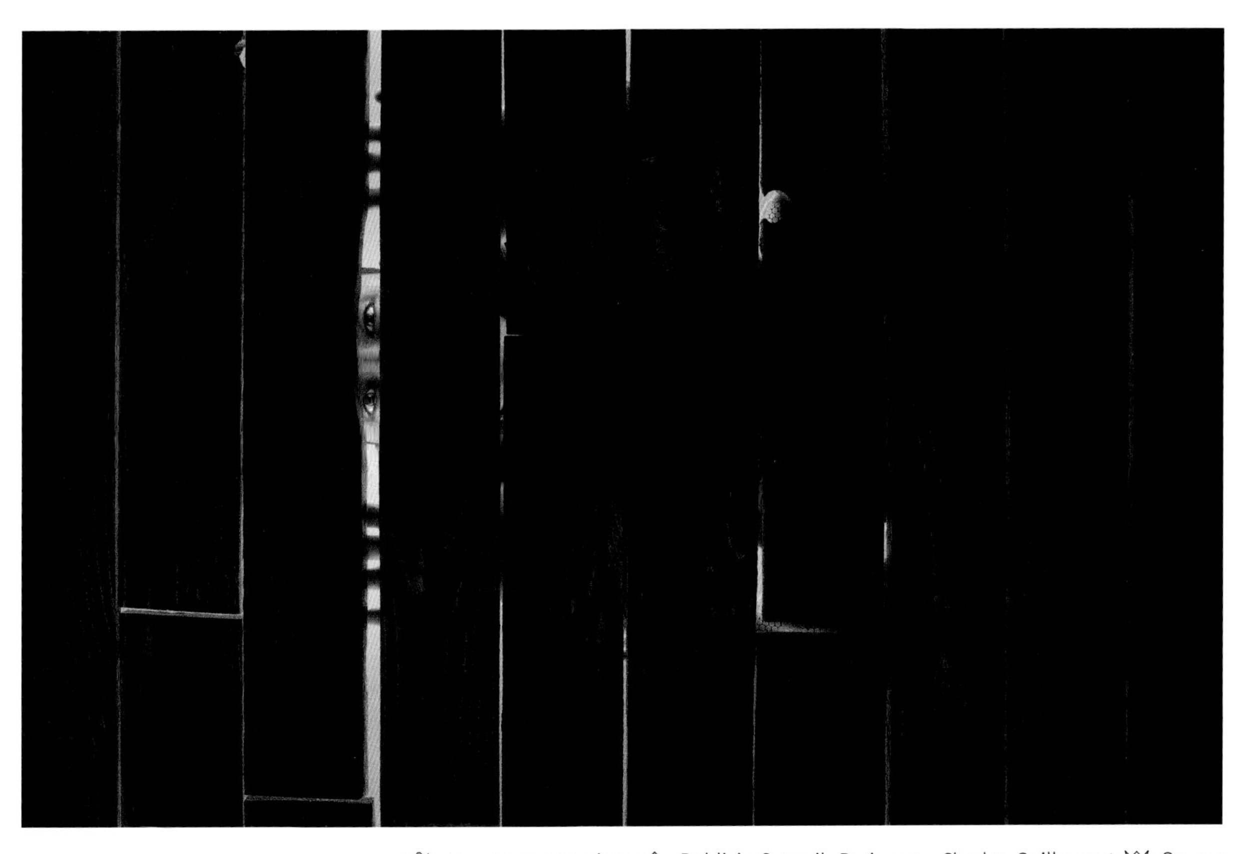

Photographer: Jean-Yves Lemoigne Agency: Publicis Conseil, Paris Art director: Charles Guillemant Client: Sagem

: David Stewart : Has Design, London : Marcus Haslam, Wesley West : Self-promotion

📷: Pawel Fabjanski ▭: Pawel Fabjanski ♕: Reporter

📷: Tony D'Orio ⌂: Blackwelk, Chicago ▭: Eric Stein, Kathy Petrauskas ♕: Chicago Canine Rescue

: Nadav Kander : TBWA, Paris : Sébastien Vacherot : Absolut Vodka

: Stewart Cohen : Samsung In-house, Richardson, Texas : Betsie Hoyt : Samsung

📷: Glen Wexler ✏: DW Pine 👑: Time Magazine

📷: Glen Wexler ✏: Cristina Scalet ♛: Time Magazine

: Stefano Gilera : United 1861, Milan : Roberto Battaglia, Federico Pepe : RTL

📷: Rogério Miranda A: Young & Rubicam, São Paulo ✏: Andre Sallowicz ♛: Santa Casa de Misericórdia de São Paulo

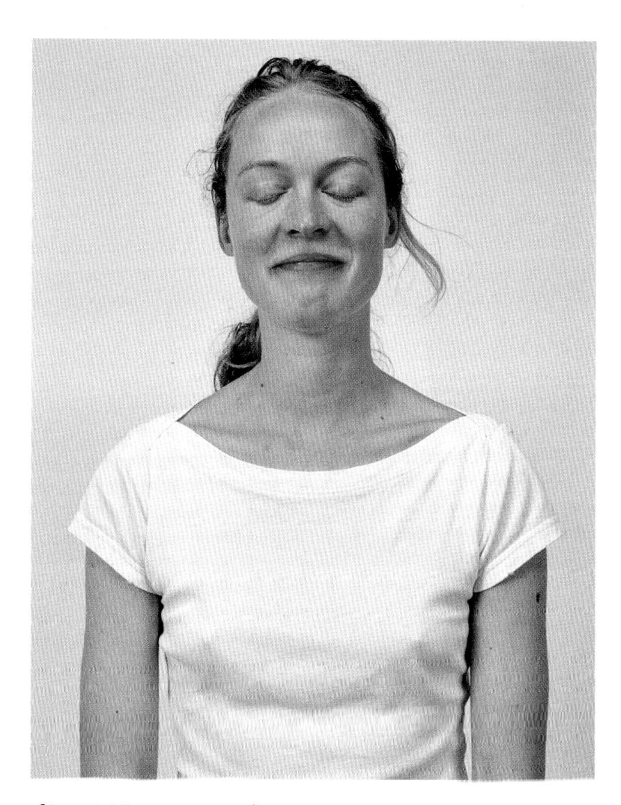

📷: Winkler & Noah A: AMD In house, Amsterdam ✏: Anne Marie Droes ♛: AMD

📷: Erik Almås ✎: Shannon Dunn ♔: 7x7 Magazine

: Erik Almås : Joey Rigg : San Francisco Chronicle

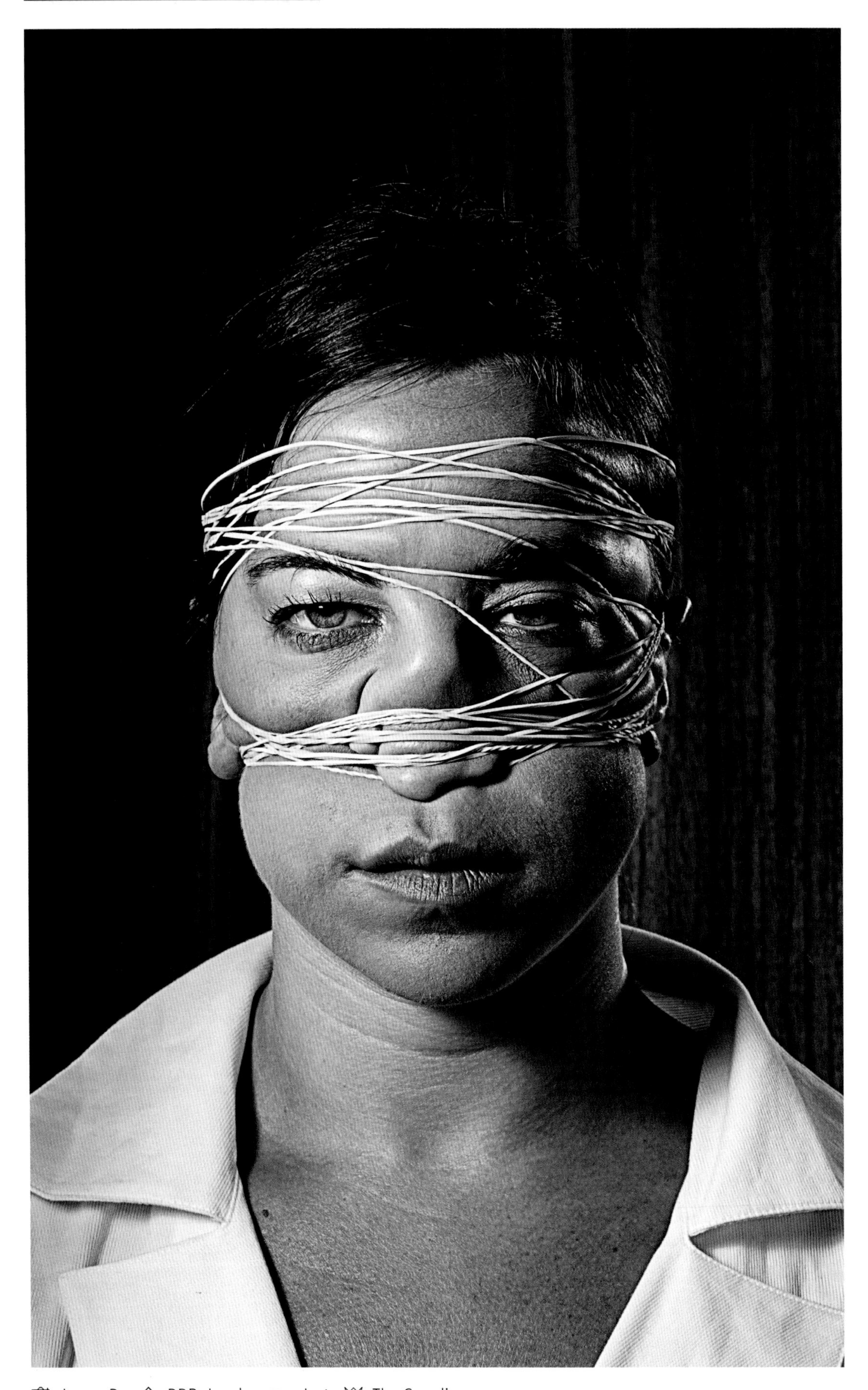

: James Day : DDB, London : Jayte : The Guardian

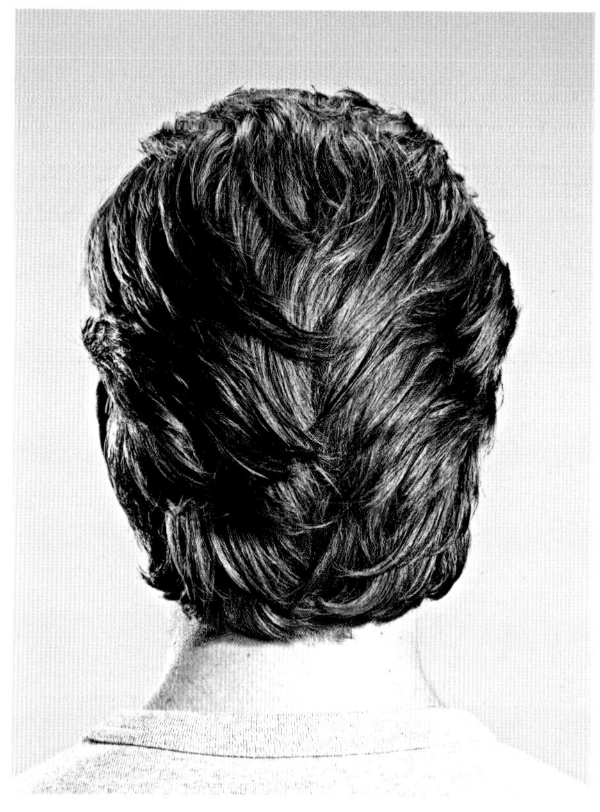

📷: James Day 👑: The New York Times

📷: RJ Muna A: FCB, Seattle ▭: Sue Boivin ♕: Nautilus

📷: Fulvio Bonavia A: mcgarrybowen, New York ▭: Haydn Morris ♕: Verizon

📷: Michael Graf ☞: Todd Cornelius ♛: Self-promotion

: Sebastian Ludvigsen : Kitchen, Oslo : Katrine Bervell : McDonald's

[camera icon]: Gerdjan van der Lugt [house icon]: Lemon Scented Tea, Amsterdam [pencil icon]: Bastiaan Rijkers [crown icon]: Krakeling

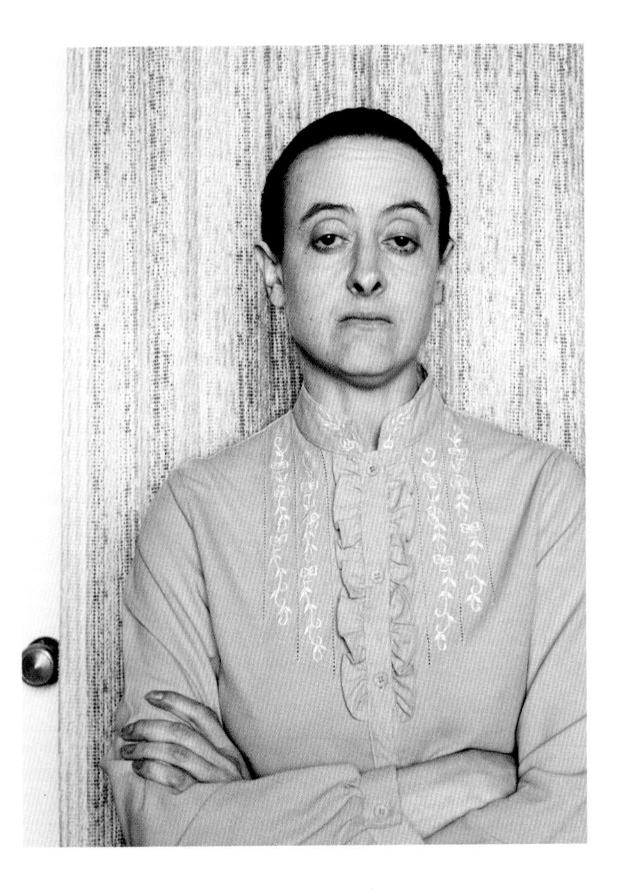

📷: Michael Corridore A: Leo Burnett, Melbourne ✎: Rob Beamish ♕: Connex

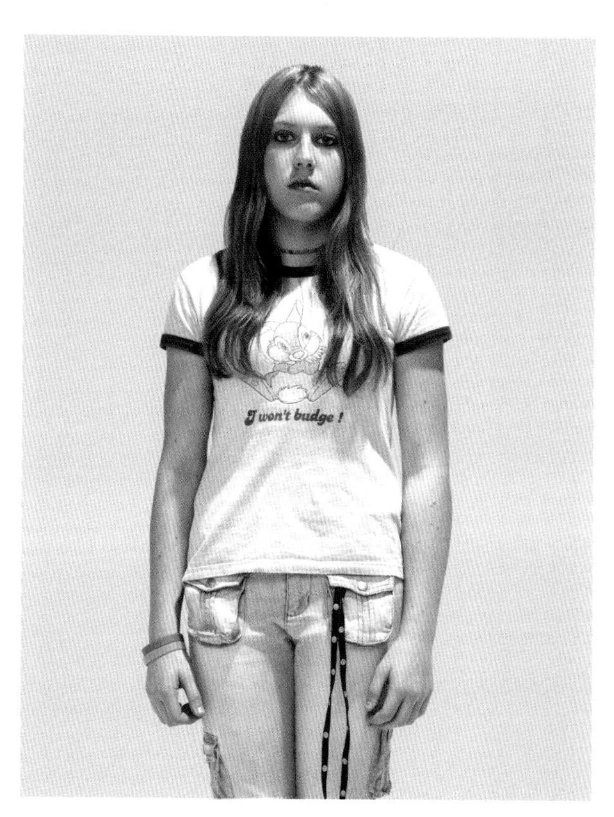

: Tony D'Orio : Self-promotion

📷: Kurt Stallaert A: Saffirio Tortelli Vigoriti, Turin ✎: Daniele Ricci ♔: Fiat

📷: David Allan Brandt A: DDB, Chicago ✎: Gary Alfredson, Eric Stein ♔: Entity

: Michael Graf : enRoute Magazine In-house, Montreal : Patrice Larose : enRoute Magazine

📷: Frank Schemmann ✎: Dieter Groll ♛: Alec Pay

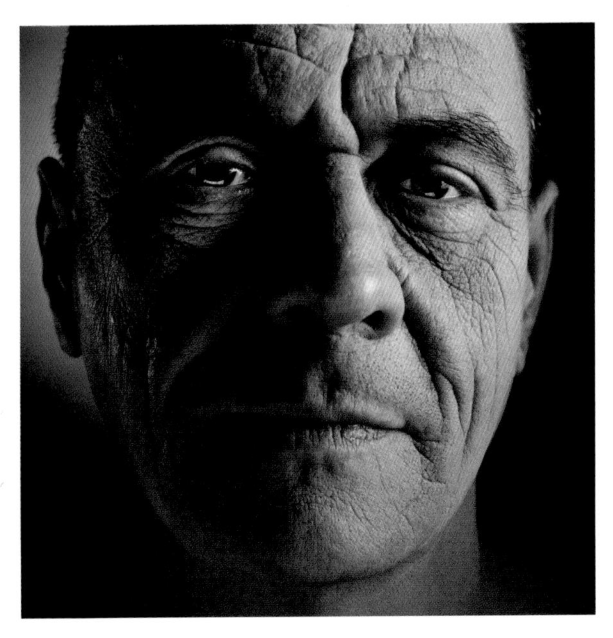

📷: Nikola Tacevski A: Young & Rubicam, Prague ✎: Lenka Sobotkova ♛: Czech Telecom

📷: Antti Viitala A: King, Helsinki ▭: Jouko Laune ♕: FRWD Outdoor Sports Computer

📷: Takahito Sato A: Daiko, Tokyo ✎: Kazunori Kitayama, Osamu Miyazaki ♕: Panasonic

📷: Takahito Sato A: Daiko, Tokyo ✏: Katunori Nishi ♔: Epson

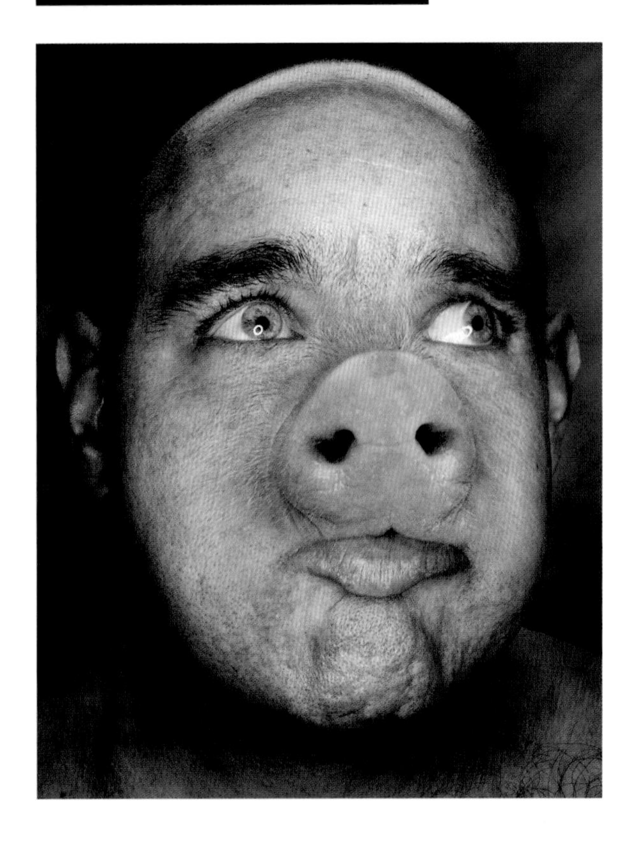

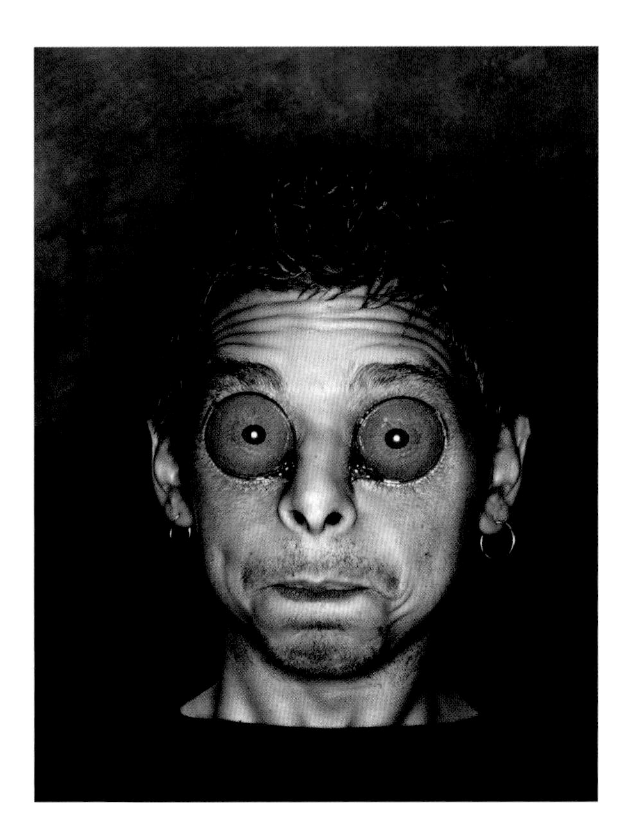

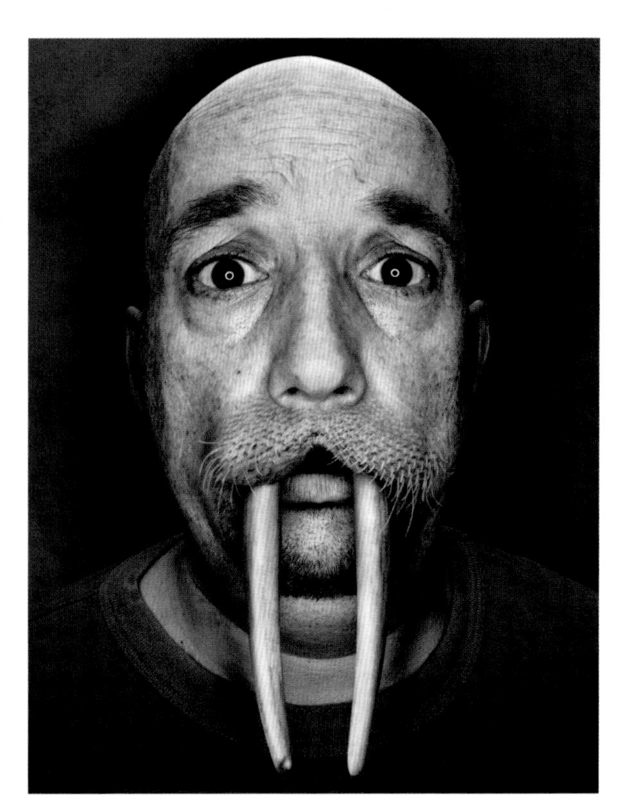

📷: Joan Garrigosa A: JWT, Barcelona ▭: Carles Puig ♕: Honda

: Leonardo Vilela : Giovanni FCB, Rio de Janeiro : Cláudio Gatao : Government of Rio de Janeiro

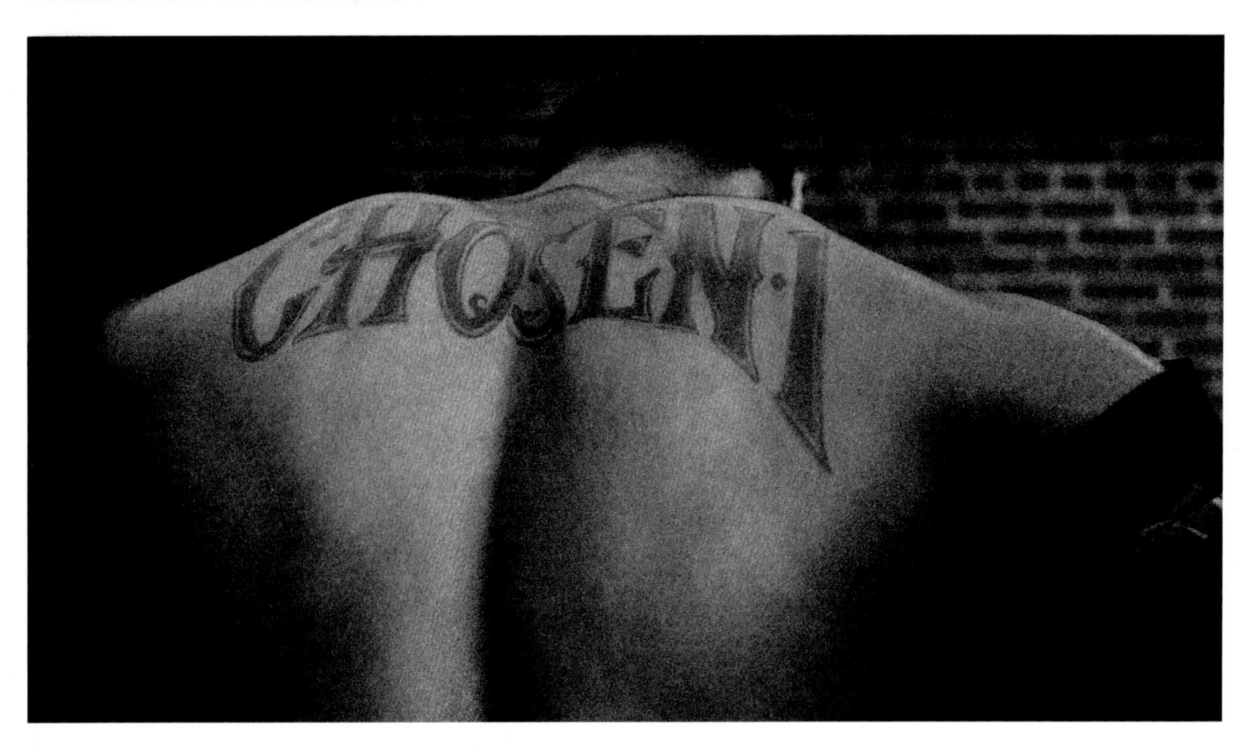

: Pier Nicola D'Amico : Michael Spoljaric : Nike

: Pier Nicola D'Amico : TracyLocke, Wilton, Connecticut : Melissa Devlin : Diet Pepsi

: Steve Bonini : adidas in-house, Portland, Oregon : Dylan Coulter : adidas

: Steve Bonini : 24 Hour Fitness

: Steve Bonini : CMD, Portland, Oregon : Alyson Taylor : Insport

📷: Erik Almås A: Nike In-house, Beaverton, Oregon ✎: Jason Herkert ♕: Nike

📷: Steve Bonini A: adidas In-house, Portland, Oregon ✎: Benjamin Wong ♕: adidas

📷: Andreas Smetana A: Publicis Mojo, Melbourne ▭: Jason Williams C: Toyota

VII

XI

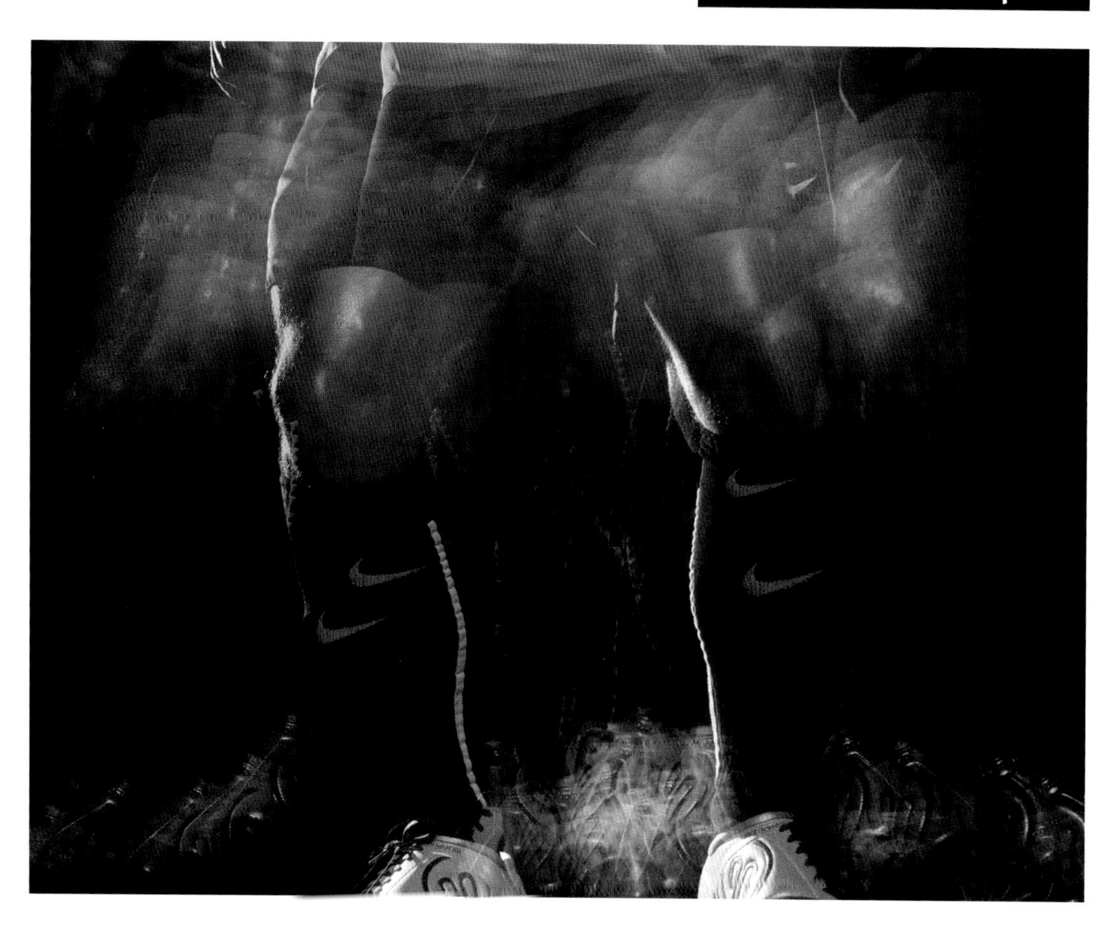

📷: Martin Sigal A: BBDO, Buenos Aires ✎: Gonzalo Vecino ♛: Nike

📷: Kurt Stallaert A: TBWA, Brussels ▭: Vital Schippers ♔: PlayStation 2

📷: Erik Almås A: Blattner Brunner, Atlanta ▭: Laura Hauseman ♔: Golf Pride

: Ross Brown : Saatchi & Saatchi, Wellington : Inia Salisbury Fisher : New Zealand Rugby Union

: Ross Brown : TBWA\Whybin, Auckland : Guy Roberts : adidas, New Zealand Rugby Union

📷: John Huet ✎: Wieden + Kennedy, Tokyo ▭: Philip Lord ♔: Nike

: John Offenbach : BETC Euro RSCG, Paris : Romain Guillon : Air France

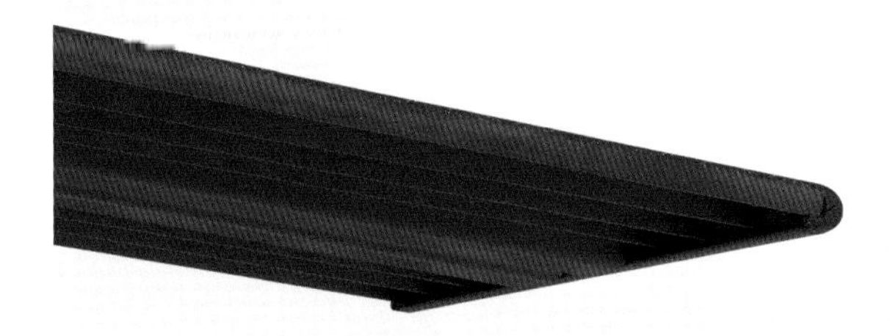

: Ricardo Miras : Atletico, Barcelona : Pablo Elorriaga : Seat

: Michael Graf : TBWA, Toronto : Jason Souce : adidas

📷: Ricardo Cunha A: Giovanni FCB, Rio de Janeiro ✍: Sergio Lobo ♕: Governo do Estado do Rio de Janeiro

📷: Thomas L. Fischer A: designafairs, Munich ✍: Mariska van Gelder, Zinaida Iller ♕: BenQ-Siemens

📷: Olaf Veltman A: Tonic, Dubai ✎: Peter Walker ♔: Dubai Sports City

📷: Jason Hindley 👑: Self-promotion

[camera]: Mark Zibert [pencil]: Erik Mohr [crown]: enRoute Magazine

[camera]: Mark Zibert [A]: TBWA, Toronto [pencil]: Mike Blanch [crown]: adidas

: Alexandre Salgado : NBS, Rio de Janeiro : André Havt : Telecine

: Alexandre Salgado : Carillo Pastore Euro RSCG, São Paulo : Marcelo Gianinni : Peugeot

: Alexandre Salgado : Young & Rubicam, São Paulo : Guilherme Somensato, Fabiano Gomes : SporTV

📷: Kai-Uwe Gundlach A: mcgarrybowen, New York ✎: Lew Willig ♔: Reebok

📷: Egon Gade ✎: Egon Gade ♕: Fritz Hansen

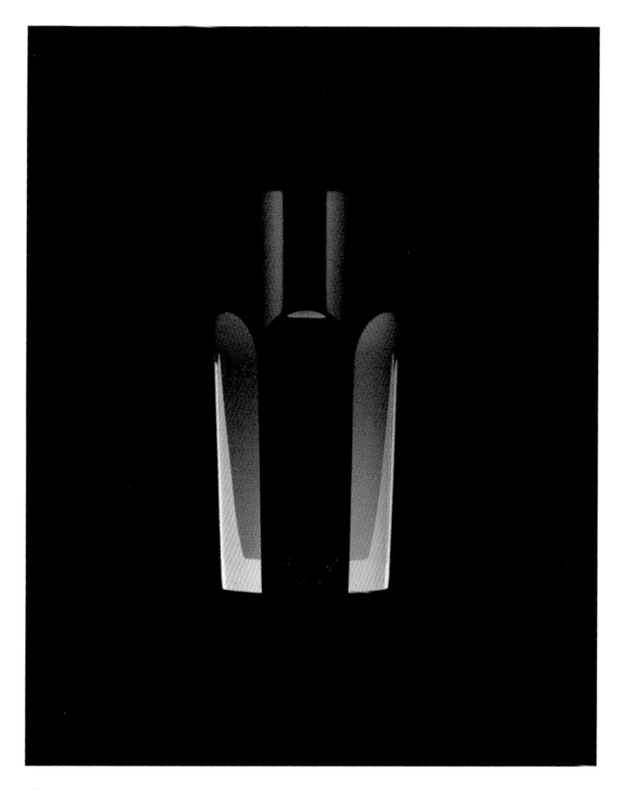

: Kenji Aoki : ATA, Tokyo : Ryoichi Shraishi : Takashimaya

: Kenji Aoki : Shogakukan In-house, Tokyo : Shogakukan

: Kenji Aoki : Shogakukan In-house, Tokyo : Shogakukan

: Kenji Aoki : Baccarat Pacific In-house, Tokyo : Baccarat Pacific

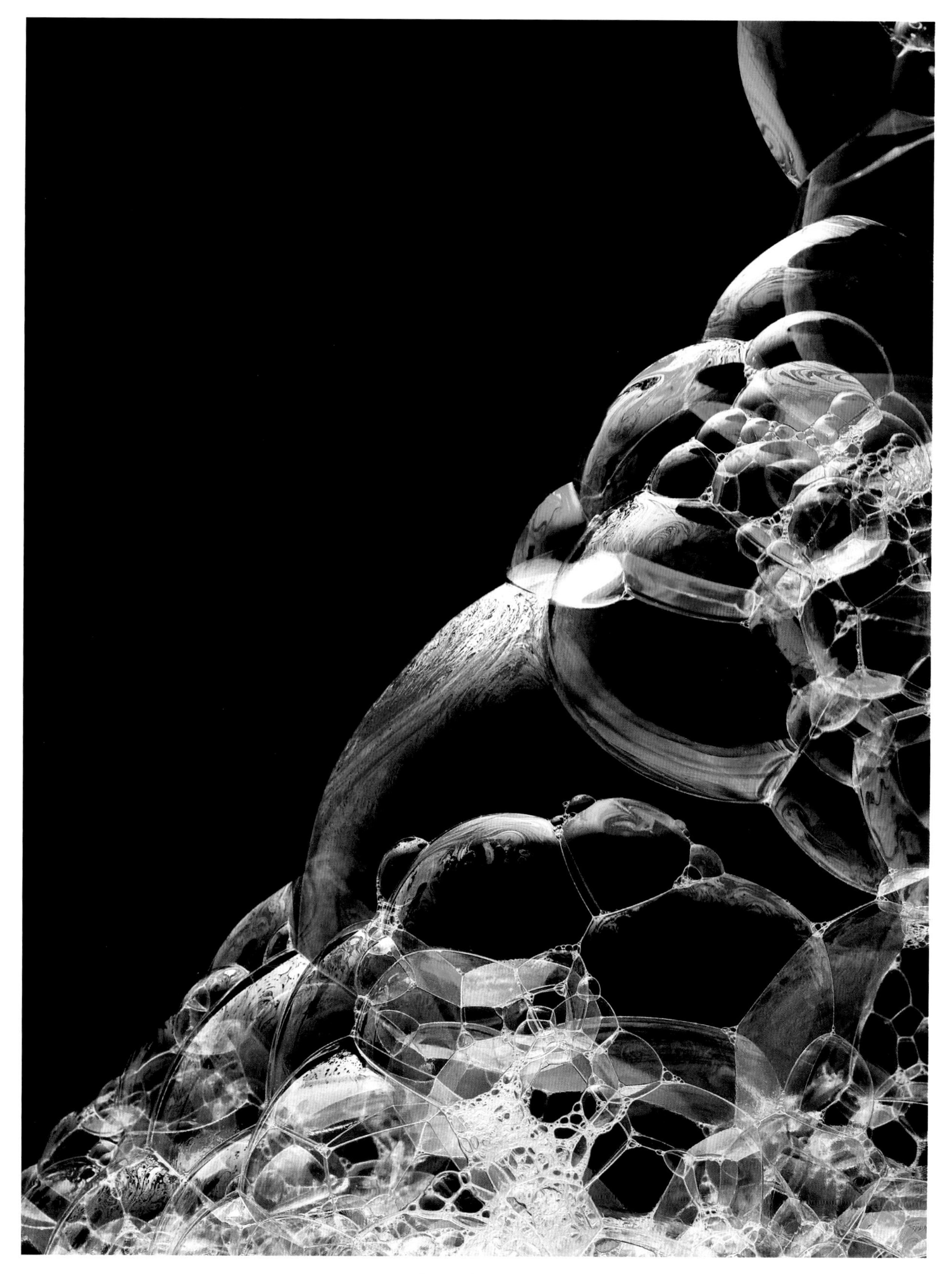

[camera]: Chai Guan Teo [agency]: JWT, Singapore [art director]: Sumesh Peringeth [client]: Persil

📷: Jillian Lochner ✏: Kirsten Lipshitz ♛: The New York Times

📷: Szeling A: Dentsu, Singapore ✎: Derek Chia ♔: Diethelm

📷: Joan Garrigosa A: JWT, Barcelona ✎: Carles Puig ♔: Harpic

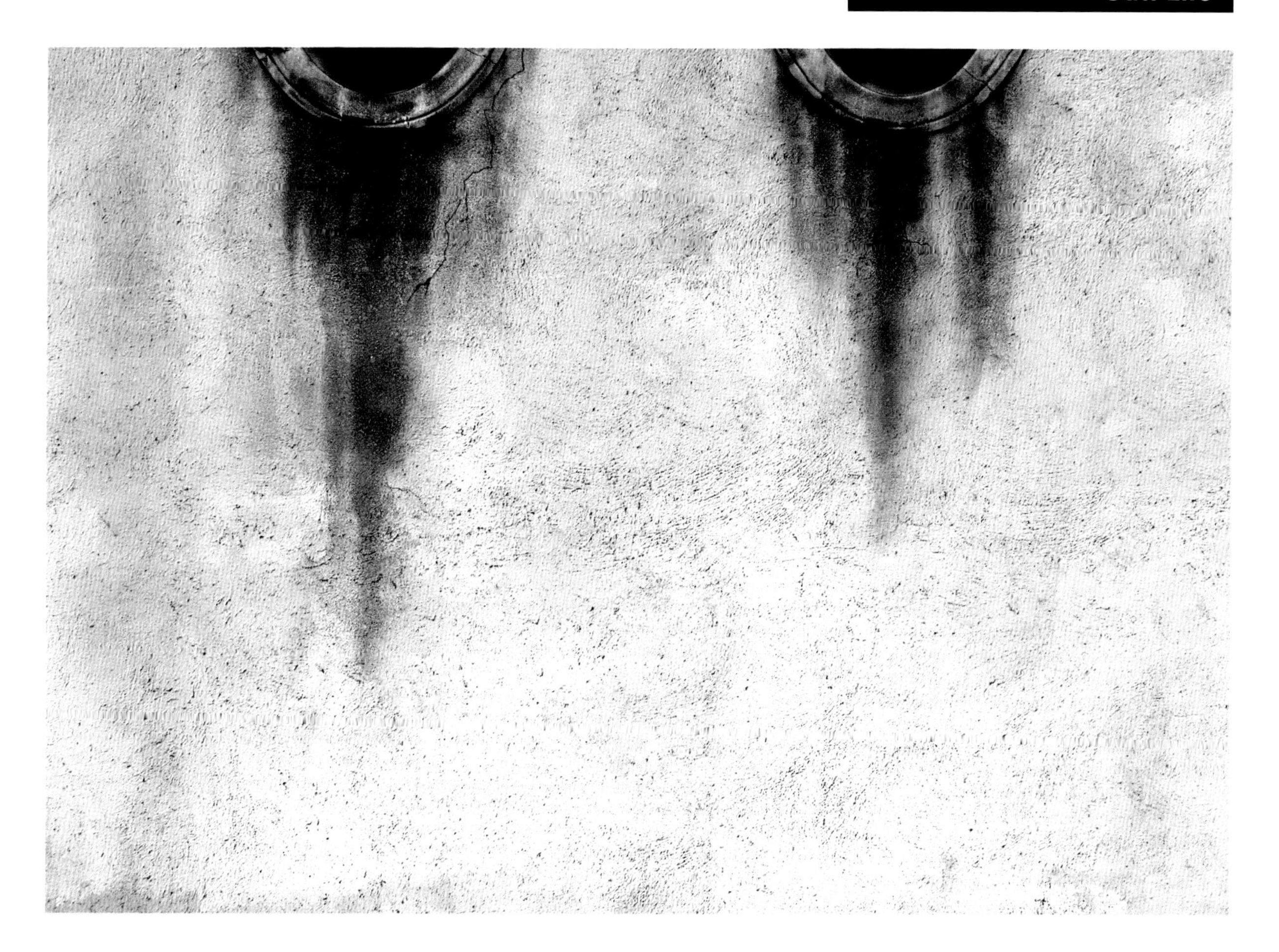

: Joan Garrigosa : JWT, Barcelona : Carles Puig : Rimmel

📷: Egon Gade A: Kunde & Co, Copenhagen ✎: Julie Secher Kau ♔: Royal Copenhagen

📷: Giblin & James A: Saatchi & Saatchi, New York ✎: Mark Voehringer ♔: Pampers

📷: Giblin & James A: Saatchi & Saatchi, New York ✎: Joseph Pompeo, James Rothwell ♔: Pampers

: Julien Vonier : Cavegnwerbung, Zurich : Markus Cavegn : Zürcher Ballett

[camera]: Christian Stoll [agency]: Ogilvy & Mather, New York [art director]: Jennifer MacFarlane [client]: IBM

[camera]: Alun Crockford [agency]: Publicis, London [art director]: Molly Godet [client]: Sofa Workshop

: Mark Laita : Eleven, San Francisco : Diane Stember : BEA Systems

: Mark Laita : Avrett Free & Ginsberg, New York : Jerry Andreozzi : Van Cleef & Arpels

📷: Mark Laita 👑: Skulls Unlimited

: Alexandre Catan : Lew Lara, São Paulo : Felipe Luchi : Tim

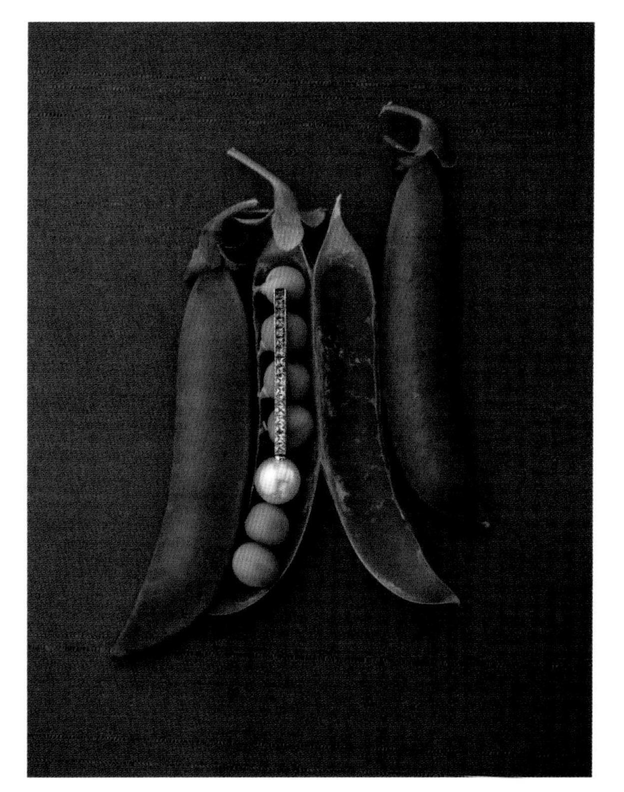

📷: Joris van Velzen 👑: Mercury

📷: Jonathan Knowles 👑: Self-promotion

📷: Jonathan Knowles A: Saatchi & Saatchi, Sydney ✎: Noah Regan 👑: Lexus

: Boudewijn Smit : Saatchi & Saatchi, Rome : Emanuele Pulvirenti : Enel

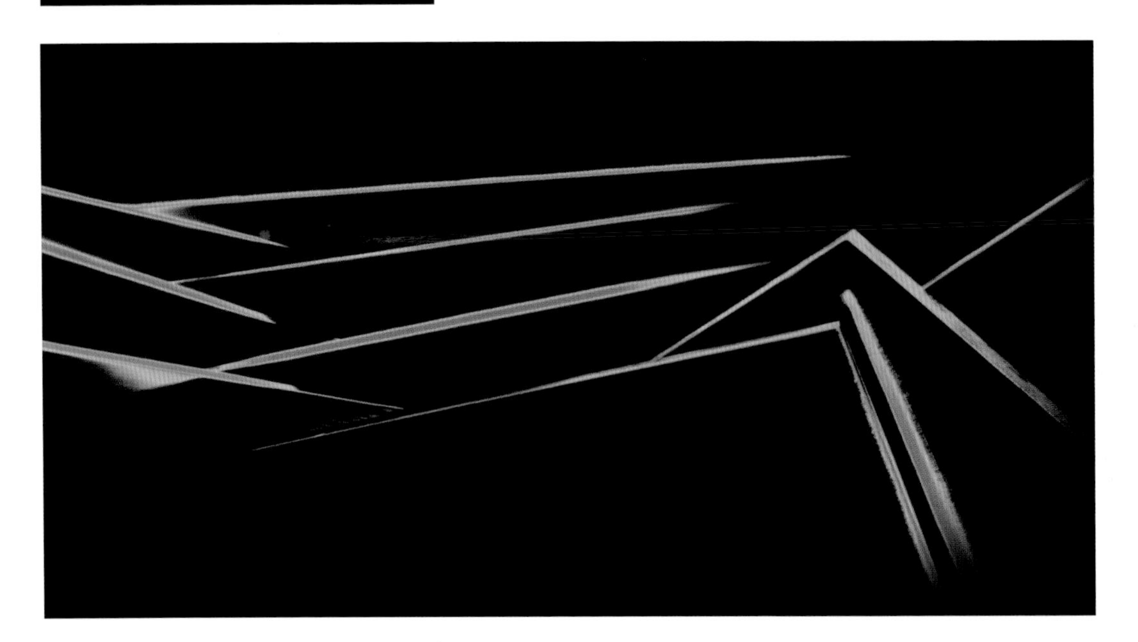

[camera icon]: Jo van den Berg [agency icon]: Ogilvy & Mather, Frankfurt am Main [pen icon]: Hermann Waterkamp [client icon]: ThyssenKrupp VDM

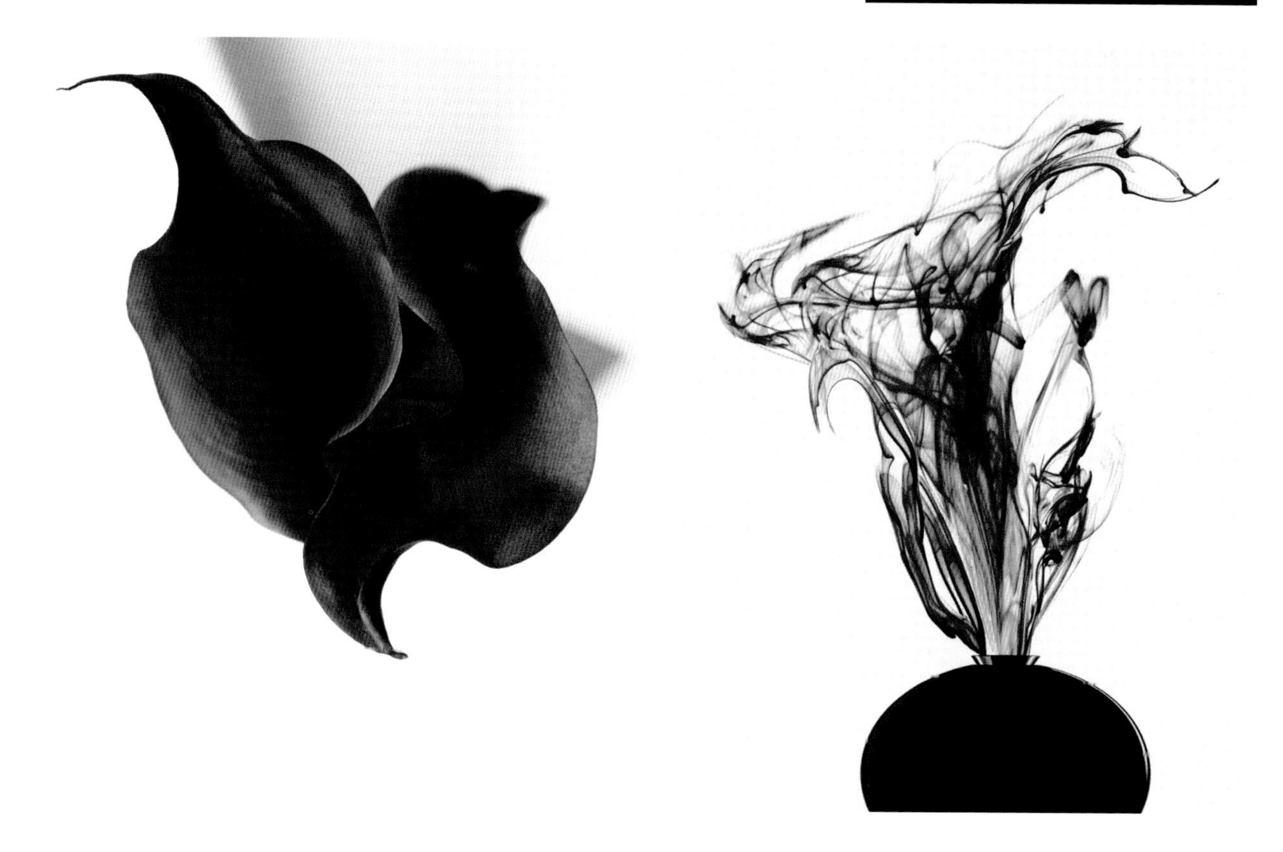

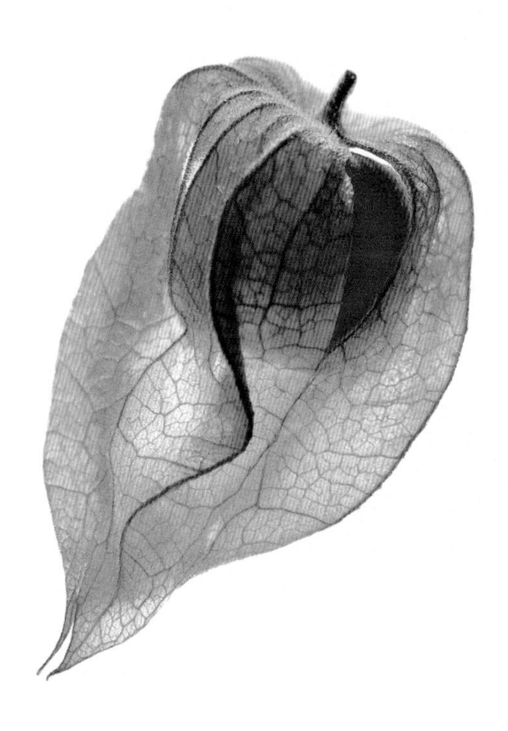

📷: Jo van den Berg ✏: Simon Ellis 👑: Schwarzkopf

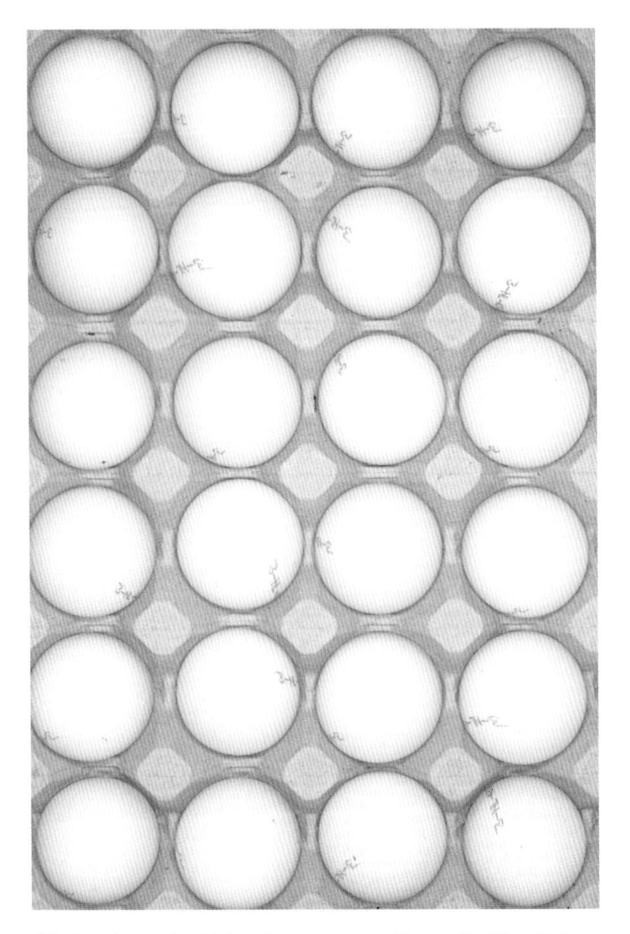

: René van der Hulst : extravers, Oisterwijk, The Netherlands : Joost Robben, Niels van Hulten : Blends

: Sergey Martiakhin : NFQ, Moscow : Andrey Klinov : Rolben

: Monzino : Inside, Milan : Monzino : Unilever

: Thomas L. Fischer : designafairs, Munich : Zinaida Iller, Mariska van Gelder : BenQ-Siemens

: Fabio Bataglia : DPZ, São Paulo : Pedro Rosa : Fuji Photo Film

📷: Vikas Dutt ♕: Avenue Engineers

📷: Vikas Dutt ♕: Adroit Solutions

📷: Stuart Crossett A: Leo Burnett, Melbourne ✎: Richard Walker, Craig Jackson ♕: Barokes

📷: Nick Vedros A: MRA, Syracuse, New York ✎: Tom Collins ♕: FedEx Kinko's

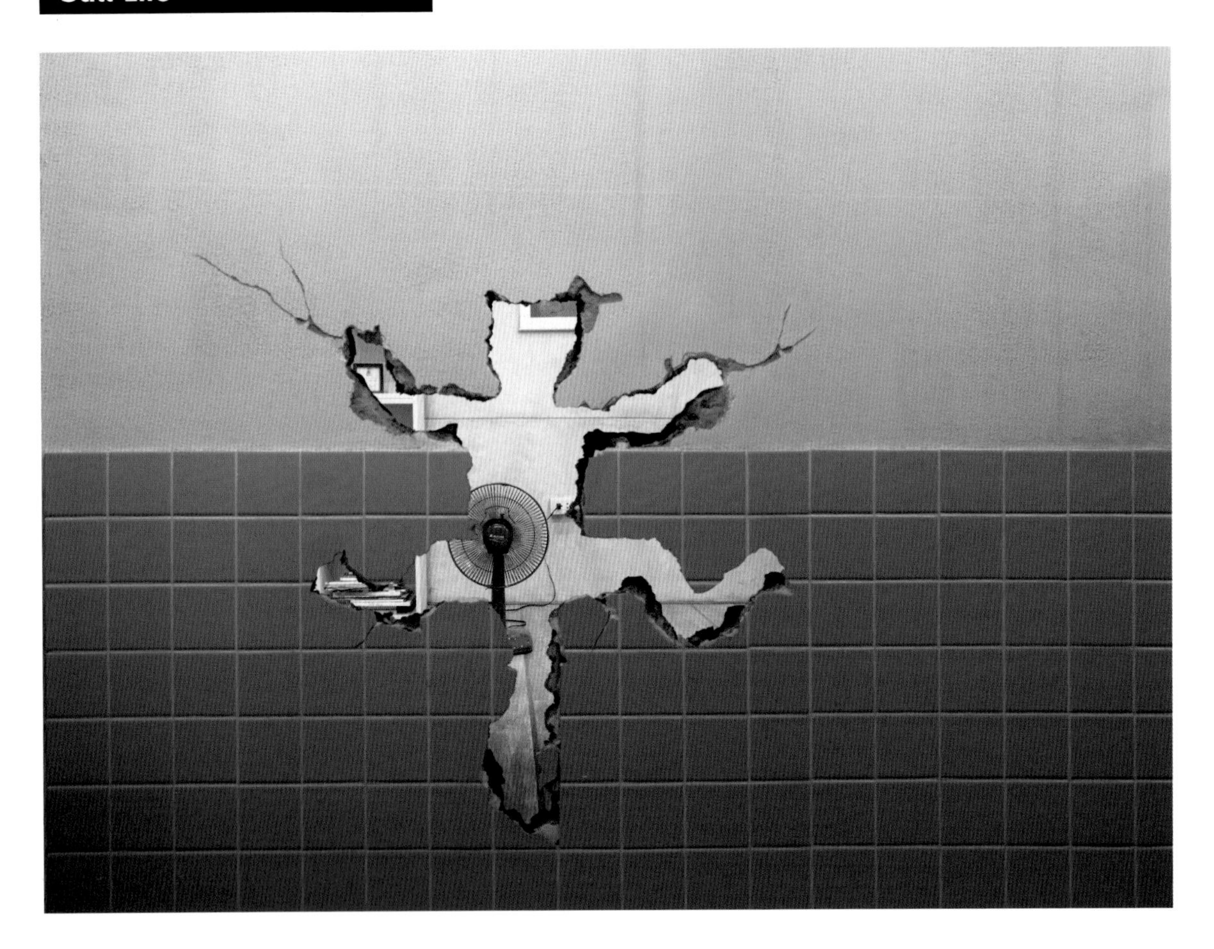

📷: Boonsunh Chalard A: BBDO, Bangkok ✎: Aniruth Assawanapanon, Vasan Wangpaitoon ♔: Accord Electric

: Simon Harsent : Publicis, New York : Alan Vladusic : Stolichnaya

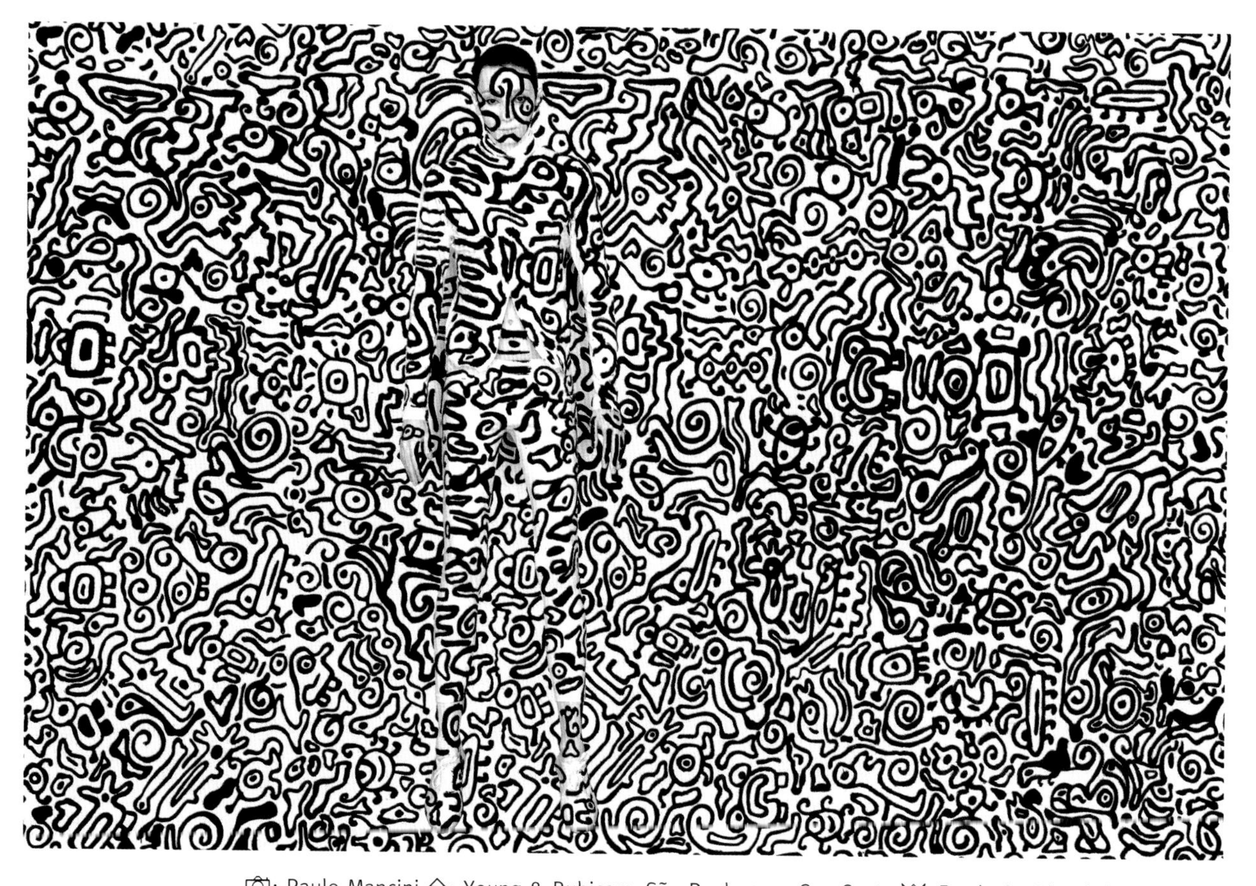

: Paulo Mancini : Young & Rubicam, São Paulo : Guy Costa : Fundação Bienal de São Paulo

📷: Rainer Stratmann A: McCann Erickson, Frankfurt am Main ✎: Andrea Abadia ♕: Opel

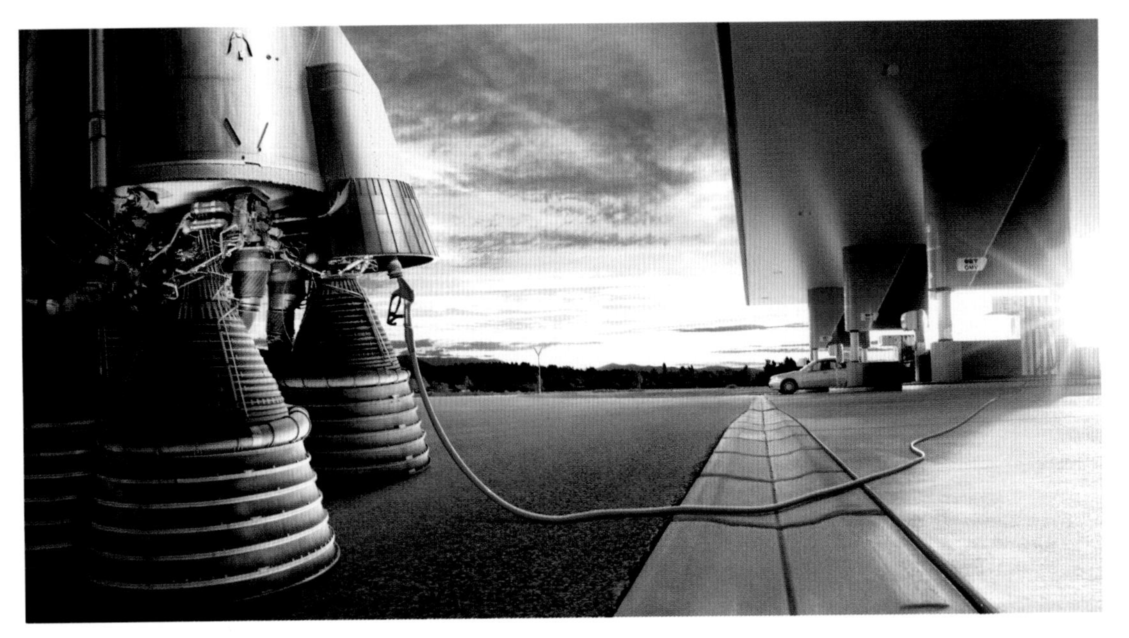

: Staudinger+Franke : Demner, Merlicek & Bergmann, Vienna : Robert Wohlgemut, Christian Bircher : OMV

: Anthony Redpath : Self-promotion

: John Offenbach : BETC Euro RSCG, Paris : Romain Guillon : Skyteam

📷: Tom Nagy A: Ogilvy & Mather, New York ▭: Jennifer MacFarlane ♕: IBM

📷: Kai-Uwe Gundlach A: Saatchi & Saatchi, Frankfurt am Main ✎: Anne Petri ♕: Audi

: Andrei Jewell : Ogilvy & Mather, Singapore : Kevin Geeves : Castrol

📷: William Huber ⌂: Nail, Providence, Rhode Island ✎: Keith Manning ♔: Atomic

📷: Simon Stock A: JWT, Houston, Texas ✏: Bob Braun ♛: Shell

📷: Kai-Uwe Gundlach A: Ringzwei, Hamburg ✎: Dirk Linke ♛: BMW

: Curtis Myers : BBDO West, San Francisco : David Swope : World War 2 Research and Preservation Society

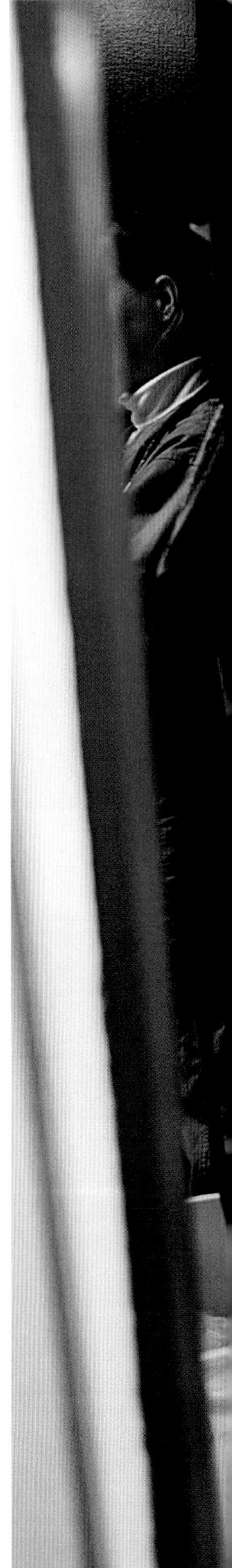

: Will van Overbeek : Trone, High Point, North Carolina : Mark Brown : Novartis Animal Health

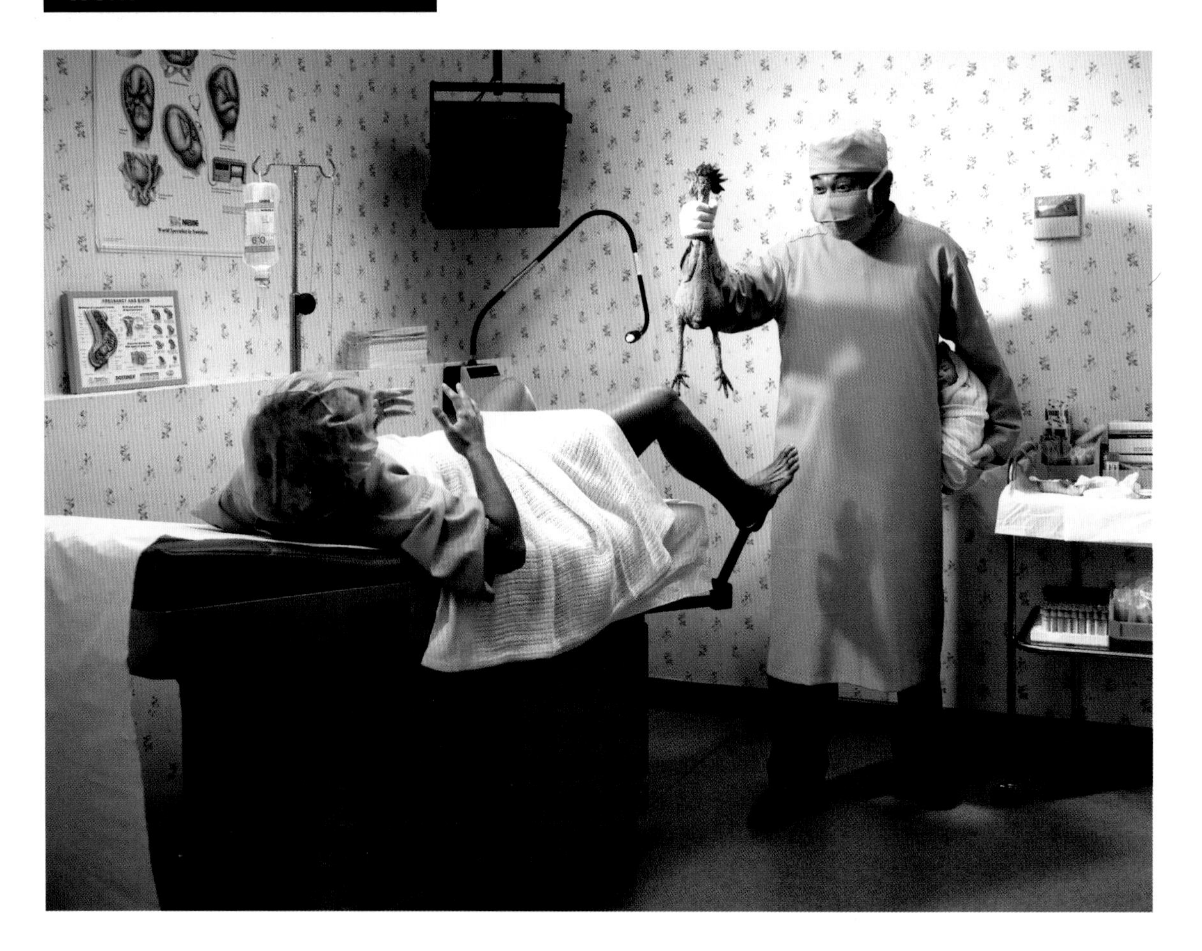

[camera]: Jonathan Tay [agency]: Saatchi & Saatchi, Singapore [art director]: Simon Cox [client]: Guinness

: Ian Butterworth : JWT, Dubai : John Foster : Mercedes-Benz

📷: Olaf Veltman 👑: Self-promotion

📷: Olaf Veltman A: Lowe, London ✏: Alistair Ross 👑: Stella Artois

📷: Marc Gouby A: Publicis Conseil, Paris ✎: Bénédicte Potel ♛: Le Sucre

📷: Jim Fiscus A: mcgarrybowen, New York ✎: Warren Eakins ♕: Reebok

📷: Jim Fiscus ✏: Larry Merritt 👑: Showtime

📷: Steve Bonini A: McClain Finlon, Denver, Colorado ✎: Mike Weed ♕: Cinch Jeans

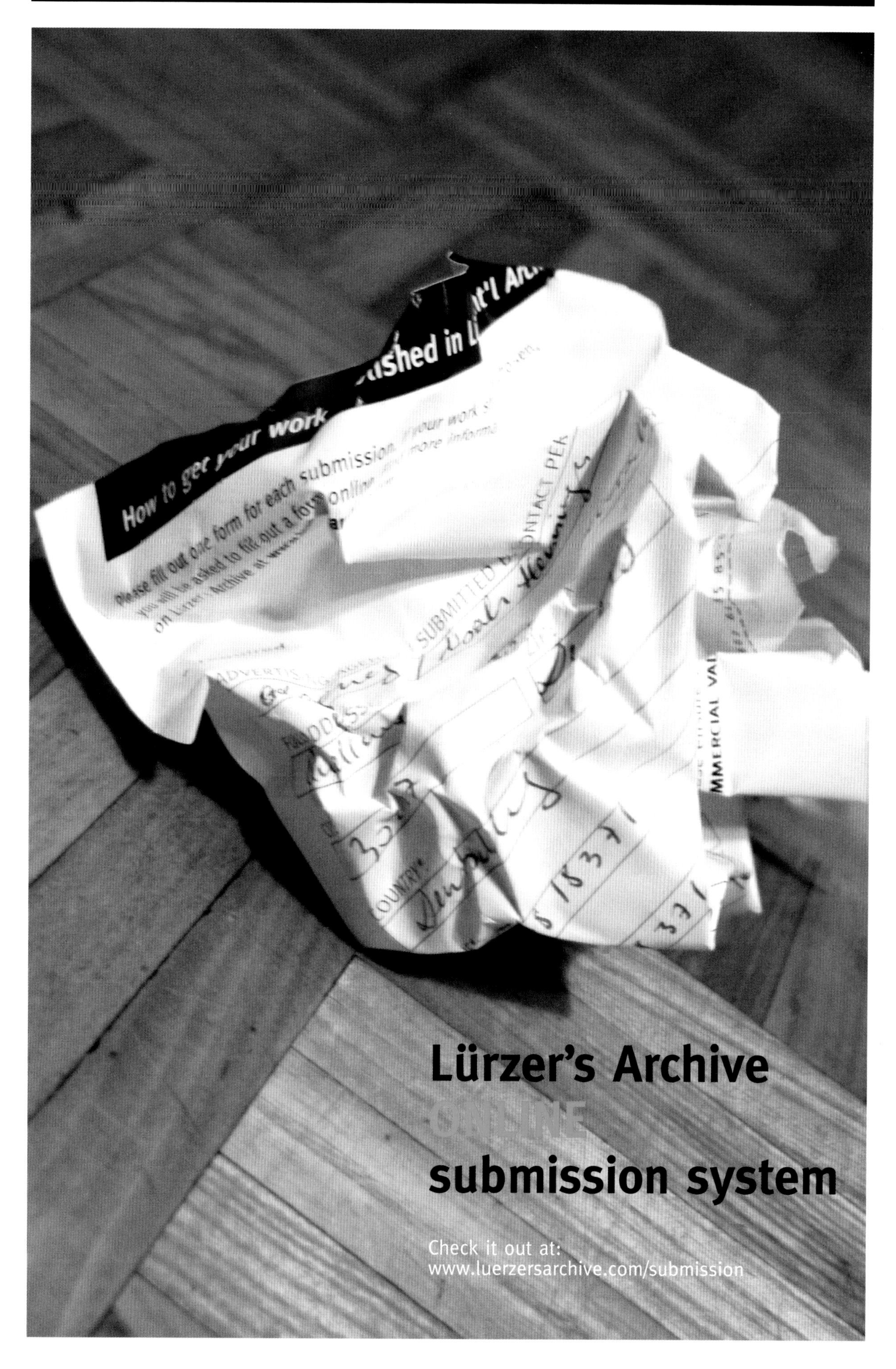
Lürzer's Archive
ONLINE
submission system
Check it out at:
www.luerzersarchive.com/submission

Crockford, Alun
London
United Kingdom
phone: (44) 20 78 37 83 38
email: alun@aluncrockford.com
www.aluncrockford.com

Crossett, Stuart
88 Inkerman Street
St. Kilda, Victoria 3182
Australia
phone: (61) 3 95 34 43 11
fax: (61) 3 95 34 11 69
email: stuart@bigstudio.com.au
www.stuartcrossett.com.au
Representative: Immik Partington
phone: (61) 417 69 99 81
www.isproduction.com.au

Cunha, Ricardo
Rua Engenheiro Pena Chaves Nº 39 Apto 102
Rio de Janeiro, RJ 22460-090
Brazil
phone: (55) 21 22 49 06 49
email: ricardo@cunhastudio.com.br
www.cunhastudio.com.br

Daan, Wendelien
Representative: Unit C.M.A.
www.unit.nl

D'Amico, Pier Nicola
700 South 10th Street, Studio 1A
Philadelphia, PY 19147
USA
phone: (1) 215 923 88 78
fax: (1) 215 923 72 44
beth@damicostudios.com
www.damicostudios.com
Representative: Deborah Ayerst
www.debayerst.com

Damon, Tim
20432 S. Santa Fe Avenue, Suite F
Carson, CA 90810
USA
phone: (1) 310 632 40 90
email: tdamonprod@aol.com
www.damonproductions.com

Day, James
83 Leonard Street
London EC2A 4QS
United Kingdom
phone: (44) 20 77 29 13 56
fax: (44) 20 77 29 08 63
email: dawn@jamesdayphoto.com
www.jamesdayphoto.com
Representative: Siobhan Squire
www.siobhansquire.com

De Villiers, Patrice
Top Floor 5 Surrey Square
London SE17 2JU
United Kingdom
phone 1: (44) 20 77 01 99 22
phone 2: (44) 77 74 13 38 49
email: patrice@patricedevilliers.com
www.patricedevilliers.com
Representative: The Carolyn Trayler Agency
phone: (44) 20 73 70 07 12
www.trayler.co.uk
Representative: Tiamat
www.tiamat.it

De Zitter, Harry
630 Lalique Circle, Unit #503
Naples, FL 34119
USA
phone: (1) 239 3 52 05 00
email: harry@dezitter.com
www.dezitter.com
Representative: Frans Kuypers
www.franskuypers.com
Representative: Nowicki's Inc.
www.nowickisinc.com

Delsaux, Cédric
33, bis avenue du Marechal Joffre
94170 Le Perreux sur Marne
France
email: cedricdelsaux@yahoo.fr
www.cedricdelsaux.com

Dixon, Vincent
31 West, 27th Street 10B
New York, NY 10001
USA
phone: (1) 212 4 81 17 28
fax: (1) 212 4 81 29 25
email: vin@vincentdixon.com
www.vincentdixon.com

D'Orio, Tony
1147 W. Ohio
Chicago, WA 60622
USA
phone: (1) 312 421 55 32
email: tony@tonydorio.com
www.tonydorio.com
Representative: Greenhouse Reps
www.greenhousereps.com

Dragan, Andrzej
Representative: Photoby
Contact: Tomasz Ireneusz Pasiek or
Krzysztof Wiecek
Dabrowiecka 6B/1
03-932 Warsaw
Poland
phone: (48) 22 618 38 18
fax: (48) 22 616 10 83
email: tomek@photoby.pl
www.photoby.pl

Dutt, Vikas
G-401, Stellar Park, Sector 62
201307 Noida
India
phone: (91) 98 10 78 32 97
email: vikas@vikasdutt.com
www.vikasdutt.com

Düttmann, Uwe
Mörikestr. 22a+b
22587 Hamburg
Germany
phone: (49) 40 86 60 06 66
fax: (49) 40 86 60 06 88
email: ud@duettmann.com
www.duettmann.com
Representative USA: Stockland Martel
phone: (1) 212 72 71 400
Representative Italy: D agency
phone: (39) 02 32 96 03 20

Eastman, Michael
6305 Westminster Pl.
St. Louis, MO 63130
USA
phone: (1) 314 863 14 00
fax: (1) 312 896 59 59
email: michael@eastmanimages.com
www.eastmanimages.com

Emmite, David
615 Se Alder #300
Portland, OR 97214
USA
phone: (1) 503 2 39 51 35
fax: (1) 503 2 39 51 70
email: david@davidemmite.com
www.davidemmite.com
Representative: Robert Mead
www.rmeadimage.com

Erickson, Jim
2 Liberty Street
Petaluma, CA 94952
USA
phone: (1) 707 7 89 04 05
fax: (1) 707 7 89 04 59
email: info@jimerickson.com
www.jimerickson.com

Fabjanski, Pawel
Representative: Photoby
Contact: Tomasz Ireneusz Pasiek or
Krzysztof Wiecek
Dabrowiecka 6B/1
03-932 Warsaw
Poland
phone: (48) 22 618 38 18
fax: (48) 22 616 10 83
email: tomek@photoby.pl
www.photoby.pl

Ferrari, Pierpaolo
Via Tertulliano 56
20137 Milan
Italy
phone: (39) 02 5 40 01 71
email: ppferrari@mac.com
Representative: Blob Creative Group
www.blobcg.com
Representative: Judy Casey
www.judycasey.com

Fischer, Thomas L.
Schulstr. 21
80634 Munich
Germany
phone: (49) 89 13 93 91 80
fax: (49) 89 13 93 91 81
email: mail@tlf.de
www.tlf.de

Fiscus, Jim
27 Waddell Street, Studio D
Atlanta, GA 30307
USA
phone: (1) 404 5 77 87 44
fax: (1) 404 4 20 29 76
email: jfiscus@fiscusphoto.com
www.fiscusphoto.com

Fitkau, Eryk
15, Simmons Street
Melbourne, Victoria 3141
Australia
phone: (61) 3 98 27 53 97
fax: (61) 3 98 24 04 83
email: info@eryk.com.au
www.eryk.com.au

Fok, Jimmy
213 Henderson Road #02-01
159553 Singapore
Singapore
phone: (65) 6 2 25 10 05
email: jimmy@calibrepics.com
www.calibrepics.com
Representative: Adrian Appel
www.katapolt.com.au

Gade, Egon
Vermundsgade 40B
2100 Copenhagen
Denmark
phone: (45) 39 27 27 12
email: egon@gadeco.dk
www.gadeco.dk

Garrigosa, Joan
C/Gaspar Fàbregas, 81
08950 Esplugues de Llobregat (Barcelona)
Spain
phone: (34) 93 3 72 03 59
email: garrigosastudio@ibernet.com
www.garrigosastudio.com

Geiss, Florian
Mueggenkampstr. 31A
20257 Hamburg
Germany
phone: (49) 40 46 00 56 50
fax: (49) 40 46 00 56 40
email: info@floriangeiss.com
www.floriangeiss.com
Representative New York: Bernstein & Andriulli
www.ba-reps.com
Representative London: Horton-Stephens
www.horton-stephens.com

Giblin & James
www.giblin-james.com
Representative UK: Agent Orange
www.agentorange.co.uk
Representative France: Anne-Marie Gardinier
www.amgardinier.com
Representative USA: Anderson Hopkins
www.andersonhopkins.com

Gilbert, Christophe
22 rue de Venise
1050 Brussels
Belgium
phone: (32) 2 6 47 76 43
fax: (32) 2 6 47 80 27
email: saga.cg@skynet.be
www.christophegilbert.com

Gilera, Stefano
Via Camerini 6
20131 Milan
Italy
email: info@stefanogilera.com
www.stefanogilera.com

Gimpel, Jefunne
Helsinki
Finland
jefunne@futureimagebank.com
www.jefunne.com
Representative: Future Image
www.futureimagebank.com

Glass, Andy
Sepham Oast, Filston Lane
Sevenoaks TN14 5JT
United Kingdom
phone: (44) 19 59 52 44 40
email: andy@andyglassphoto.com
www.andyglassphoto.com
Representative: Robin Dictenberg
www.greenhousereps.com
Representative: Wyatt Clarke
www.wyattclarke.com

Gobits, Rolph
Representative: Stockland Martel
5 Union Square West, 6th Floor
New York, NY 10003
phone: (1) 212 727 14 00
email: talentinfo@stocklandmartel.com
www.stocklandmartel.com

Gouby, Marc
9 rue du Père Brottier
75016 Paris
France
phone: (33) 1 42 24 09 67
www.marcgouby.com
Representative: Maureen Sale
email: contact@maureensale.com
www.maureensale.com

Graf, Michael
33 Davies Avenue
Toronto, ON M4M 2A9
Canada
phone: (1) 416 4 62 09 50
fax: (1) 416 4 62 13 24
email: info@grafstudios.com
www.grafstudios.com

Gundlach, Kai-Uwe
Arndtstr. 24a
22085 Hamburg
Germany
phone: (49) 40 61 01 89
fax: (49) 40 61 02 13
email: info@studiogundlach.de
www.studiogundlach.de
Representative: Stockland Martel
www.stocklandmartel.com

Hajdu, Andràs
Karinthy Frigyes út 3
1117 Budapest
Hungary
phone: (36) 30 9 34 16 60
email: hajduandras@yahoo.com
Representative: PhotoPro
www.photopro.hu

Haksar, Sharad
3, 1st Floor, 1st Main Road, Seethammal Extension
600018 Chennai
India
phone: (91) 44 24 31 48 41
fax: (91) 44 24 31 48 43
email: sharad@sharadhaksar.com
www.sharadhaksar.com

Hall, Stuart
email: stuarthallphoto@gmail.com
www.stuarthallphoto.com
Representative: Marilyn Cadenbach
marilyn@cadenbach.com
www.cadenbach.com

Hänel, Johann Sebastian
Torstr. 220
10115 Berlin
Germany
phone: (49) 172 1 75 63 84
email: sebastian@pronet.hu
www.johannsebastianhanel.com
Representative: PAM
www.pam-hamburg.de

Hanzawa, Takeshi
1-17-4 Shibuya Estate Bldg. 705, Shibuya,
Shibuya-ku
Tokyo 150-0002
Japan
phone: (81) 3 34 86 56 77
fax: (81) 3 34 86 56 78
email: info@cubetokyo.com
www.earthpipe.com

Harsent, Simon
44 West 18th Street
New York, NY 10011
USA
phone: (1) 212 6 47 03 36
email: harsent@mac.com
www.simonharsent.com
Representative: Monaco Reps
www.monacoreps.com

Herholdt, Frank
15 Gascoigne Place
London E2 7LY
United Kingdom
phone: (44) 20 76 13 34 24
email: info@frankherholdt.com
www.frankherholdt.com
Representative: Agent Orange
www.agentorange.co.uk
Representative: Judith Miller
www.judithmillerinc.com

Hindley, Jason
www.jasonhindley.com
Representative UK: Agent Orange
www.agentorange.co.uk
Representative France: Anne-Marie Gardinier
www.amgardinier.com
Representative USA: Anderson Hopkins
www.andersonhopkins.com

Hirano, Kousaku
405 Takano Bldg. 2-13-19 Minami-azabu, Minato-ku
Tokyo 106-0047
Japan
phone: (81) 3 34 52 27 85
fax: (81) 3 58 56 88 60
email: corabo@lake.ocn.ne.jp
www.kyosel-genkai.org

Hirit, Gabi
Tepes Voda
21521 Bucharest
Romania
phone: (40) 2 13 23 50 98
email: gabi@hirit.ro
www.gabihirit.com

Ho, Lewis
2/F Warner Bldg., 89 Hennessy Road, Wanchai
Hong Kong
China
phone: (852) 25 28 20 07
fax: (852) 28 04 21 92
email: fbilulu@netvigator.com
www.studioinclineltd.com.hk

Holloway, Zena
8 Avenue Crescent
London W3 8EW
United Kingdom
phone: (44) 20 89 93 99 50
email: zena@gotadsl.co.uk
www.zenaholloway.com
Representative: The Peter Bailey Company
www.peterbailey.co.uk

Hong, Connie
Unit 2207, Westlands Centre,
20 Westlands Road, Quarry Bay
Hong Kong
China
phone: (852) 24 22 21 68
fax: (852) 25 63 66 28
email: info@ki-photography.com
www.ki-photography.com

Huber, William
355 Congress Street, Fl. 2
Boston, MA 02210
USA
phone: (1) 617 2 02 95 16
fax: (1) 617 8 48 12 01
email: info@williamhuber.com
www.williamhuber.com
Representative: Marilyn Cadenbach
www.cadenbach.com

Huet, John
P.O. Box 1506
Manchester, MA 01944
USA
phone: (1) 978 5 26 00 50
email: jhuet@redcatpro.com
www.johnhuet.com
Representative: Marilyn Cadenbach
www.cadenbach.com

Hylén, Bo
Representative Germany: Christa Klubert
phone: (49) 211 5 57 06 06
email: mail@christaklubert.com
www.christaklubert.com
Representative USA: Marsha Fox (Fox Creative)
phone: (1) 323 8 45 17 60
email: marsha@foxcreative.net

Izzard, Sean
219 Enmore Road
Enmore, NSW 2042
Australia
phone: (61) 2 95 65 40 11
fax: (61) 2 95 65 40 17
email: sean@seanizzard.com
www.seanizzard.com
Representative: Kirsty Meares
www.kirstymeares.com

Jewell, Andrei
phone: (64) 2 74 97 17 06
email: gaiafilm@ihug.co.nz
www.andreijewell.com

Kander, Nadav
Unit D, Imperial Works, Perren Street
London NW5 3ED
United Kingdom
email: [illegible]
www.nadavkander.com
Representative: Stockland Martel
www.stocklandmartel.com

Kantor, Jonathan
195 Hudson St #4-E
New York, NY 10013
USA
phone: (1) 212 343 02 52
email: jon@jonathankantor.com
www.jonathankantor.com
Representative: Monaco Reps
www.monacoreps.com

Kars, Edo
Kerkstraat 111
1017 GD Amsterdam
The Netherlands
phone: (31) 20 6 39 12 22
fax: (31) 20 6 39 16 80
email: thomas@karsphotography.nl
www.edokars.com
Representative: Marilyn Cadenbach
www.cadenbach.com
Representative: Maureen Sale
www.maureensale.com
Representative: Tiamat
www.tiamat.lt

Karsten, Dirk
Pekkendam 8
1081 HR Amsterdam
The Netherlands
phone: (31) 20 6 97 21 41
email: dirkkarsten@dirkkarsten.com
www.dirkkarsten.com
Representative Italy: Hilary Bradford
www.hilarybradford.com
Representative UK and France: Valerie Hersleven
www.valeriehersleven.com

Keil, Peter
Hansaallee 159
40549 Düsseldorf
Germany
phone: (49) 211 90 17 50
fax: (49) 211 39 41 71
email: peter@keil-photography.com
www.keil-photography.com

Kern, Geof
Representative: Friend & Johnson
443 Greenwich St #6J
New York, NY 10013
USA
phone: (1) 212 3 37 00 55
email: geof@geofkern.com
www.geofkern.com

Kifert, Kasia
Representative: Photoby
Contact: Tomasz Ireneusz Pasiek or
Krzysztof Wiecek
Dabrowiecka 6B/1
03-932 Warsaw
Poland
phone: (48) 22 618 38 18
fax: (48) 22 616 10 83
tomek@photoby.pl
www.photoby.pl

Kniat, Norbert
Liniengasse 2b/4
1060 Wien
Austria
phone: (43) 1 5 95 61 39
email: norbert@kniat.de
www.kniat.de
Representative: Joe Berger
www.joe-berger.com
Representative: Andrea Walji
www.andreawalJI.com

Knowles, Jonathan
48A Chancellors Road
London W6 9RS
United Kingdom
phone: (44) 20 87 41 75 77
email: jk@jknowles.com
www.jknowles.com

Lahdesmaki, Markku
see under "Markku"

Laita, Mark
3815 Main Street
Culver City, CA 90232
USA
phone: (1) 310 8 36 16 45
fax: (1) 310 8 36 03 45
email: mark@marklaita.com
www.marklaita.com

Lauritzen, Mads
Frederiksborg 1A, 4th Floor
1360 Copenhagen
Denmark
phone: (45) 20 85 48 88
email: mads@lauritzen.dk
www.madslauritzen.com

Law, Wher
Workshop 1202, Chai Wan Industrial City 2, 70 Wing
Tai Road, Chai Wan
Hong Kong
China
phone: (852) 2 5 16 65 11
fax: (852) 2 5 16 65 27
email: wherstud@netvigator.com
www.wherlawstudio.com

Lemoigne, Jean-Yves
73, Rue Saint Maur
75011 Paris
France
phone: (33) 6 63 48 33 20
email: contact@jeanyveslemoigne.com
www.jeanyveslemoigne.com
Representative: Bransch
www.bransch.net

Leverman, Peter
6060 Coburg Road
Halifax, Nova Scotia B3H 1 Z2
Canada
phone: (1) 902 4 31 63 99
email: peter@peterleverman.com
www.peterleverman.com

Lewis, Michael
Representative: Rob Lawrence
www.studiorproductions.com
Representative: Cecile Rodrigue
www.cecilerodrigue.com
Representative: Robin Dictenberg
www.greenhousereps.com

Lochner, Jillian
61 Malmesbury Road, Bow
London E3 2EB
United Kingdom
phone: (44) 77 95 41 16 82
email: info@jillianlochner.com
www.jillianlochner.com
Representative: Germaine Walker
www.germaine.co.uk
Representative: John Kenny & Associates
www.Jkand.com

Ludvigsen, Sebastian
Gøteborggata 27b
0566 Oslo
Norway
phone: (47) 93 03 23 32
email: sebastian@sebastianludvigsen.com
www.sebastianludvigsen.com

Magg, Ari
Hverfisgötu 18a
101 Reykjavik
Iceland
phone: (354) 5 61 96 90
email: ari@magg.com
www.arimagg.com
Representative: MAGG
www.magg.is

Manarchy, Dennis
656 W Hubbard St
Chicago, IL 60610
USA
phone: (1) 312 6 66 74 00
fax: (1) 312 6 66 24 00
www.manarchy.com
Representative: @radical.media
http://photo.radicalmedia.com

Mancini, Paulo
Rua Prof. José Leite e Oiticica, 207 Vila Gertrudes
São Paulo, SP 04705-080
Brazil
phone: (55) 11 55 05 69 00
email: paulo_mancini@uol.com.br
www.paulomancini.com.br

Markku – Markku Lahdesmaki
23400 Moon Shadows Drive
Malibu, CA 90265
USA
phone: (1) 310 4 56 69 64
fax: (1) 310 3 17 95 49
email: markku@earthlink.net
www.markkuphoto.com
Representative: Veronique Roc
www.veroniqueroc.com
Representative: @radical.media
http://photo.radicalmedia.com

Martiakhin, Sergey
Udalcova 69a, 58
113454 Moscow
Russia
phone: (7) 95 7 60 69 82
fax: (7) 95 9 78 01 83
email: info@studiomart.ru
www.studiomart.ru

McFetridge, Alan
Representative USA: Anderson Hopkins
phone: (1) 212 43 15 117
email: steph@andersonhopkins.com
www.andersonhopkins.com
Representative Australia & Asia: Look
phone: (61) 2 93 80 88 22
email: mark@lookproductions.com
www.lookproductions.com
Representative New Zealand: Match Photographers
phone: (64) 9 37 88 572
email: gerardine@matchphotographers.com
www.matchphotographers.com

Salgado, Alexandre
Rua Teotonio Regadas 26, Sala 803
Rio de Janeiro, RJ 20021-360
Brazil
phone: (55) 21 22 21 11 19
email: artluzstudio@artluzstudio.com.br
www.artluzstudio.com.br

Salzano, James
29 West 15th Street
New York, NY 10011
USA
phone: (1) 212 2 42 48 20
email: js@salzanophoto.com
www.salzanophoto.com
Representative: Marianne Campbell
www.mariannecampbell.com

Sato, Takahito
Minami-Aoyama 5-3-8, Palace Miyuki #702,
Minato-ku
Tokyo 107-0062
Japan
phone: (81) 3 34 00 10 11
fax: (81) 3 54 69 53 28
email: beam@sato.email.ne.jp
[illegible]

Schaffer, Rodney
Level 1, 88 Inkerman Street
St. Kilda, Victoria 3182
Australia
phone: (61) 3 95 34 43 11
email: rod@bigstudio.com.au
www.rodschaffer.com
Representative: Contacts
www.contacts-pro.com.au
Representative: Stone Camera
www.stonecamera.com

Schatz, Howard
435 West Broadway
New York, NY 10012
USA
phone: (1) 212 3 34 66 67
fax: (1) 212 3 34 66 69
www.howardschatz.com
Representative: Beverly Ornstein
email: beverly@howardschatz.com

Scheffold.Vizner
Zypressenstr. 85
8004 Zurich
Switzerland
phone: (41) 44 2 40 17 40
email: contact@scheffold.vizner.com
www.scheffold.vizner.com

Schemmann, Frank
Bilkerstr. 23
40213 Düsseldorf
Germany
phone: (49) 211 7 33 30 80
fax: (49) 211 7 33 30 81
email: studio@schemmann.com
www.schemmann.com
Representative: Rockenfeller & Göbels
www.fotografen-agentur.de

Schlatter, Robert
1 Clarence Place, #10
San Francisco, CA 94107
USA
phone: (1) 415 2 84 08 30
fax: (1) 415 2 84 09 30
www.robertschlatter.com
Representative: @radical.media
http://photo.radicalmedia.com

Schmidt, Christian
Silberburgstr. 119A
70176 Stuttgart
Germany
phone: (49) 711 6 15 11 33
email: info@christianschmidt.com
www.christianschmidt.com
Representative USA: @radical.media
http://photo.radicalmedia.com
Representative Germany: Claudia Bitzer
www.claudiabitzer.de

Schmidt, Heimo
P.O. Box 972
Sausalito, CA 94966
USA
phone: (1) 415 7 89 18 48
email: heimo@rcn.com

Schnabel, Michael
Höhenstr. 5
73269 Hochdorf
Germany
phone: (49) 7153 92 29 86
fax: (49) 7153 92 29 87
email: mail@michael-schnabel.com
www.michaelschnabel.com
[illegible]
[illegible]
Representative: Bernstein & Andriulli
www.ba-reps.com
Representative: Valerie Hersleven
www.valeriehersleven.com

Scholten, Jan Willem
KNSM-laan 73
1019 LB Amsterdam
The Netherlands
phone: (31) 20 3 44 50 30
fax: (31) 20 3 44 50 38
email: studio@jwsfoto.nl
www.jwsfoto.nl

Seaward, Pete
phone: (44) 20 72 42 00 24
email: sue@sueallott.com
Representative: Sue Allott
www.peteseaward.com

Secharunputong, Anuchai
c/o Remix Studio
Ladprao 94
Bangkok 10310
Thailand
phone: (66) 2 9 35 60 18
fax: (66) 2 9 35 69 01
email 1: remix_th@yahoo.com
email 2: remix_sct2@yahoo.com

Serrano, Ramón
Madrazo, 54
8006 Barcelona
Spain
phone: (34) 93 2 09 01 69
fax: (34) 93 4 14 59 50
email: ramonstudio@ramonstudio.com
www.ramonstudio.com

Siah, Sebastian
136 Joo Seng Road, 1st Fl. Brilliant Bldg.
Singapore 368360
Singapore
phone: (65) 62 89 88 28
fax: (65) 62 89 88 18
email: sebsiah@shootinggalleryasia.com
Representative: Shooting Gallery
www.shootinggalleryasia.com

Sigal, Martin
Bolivia 3589
Buenos Aires, C1419 DTA
Argentinia
phone: (54) 11 45 73 41 59
fax: (54) 11 45 71 55 98
email: sigal@sigalfotografia.com.ar
www.sigalfotografia.com.ar

Simhoni, George
70 Ward Street
Toronto, ON M6H 4A6
Canada
phone: (1) 416 5 35 19 55
email: george@westsidestudio.com
www.georgesimhoni.com
Representative: Westside Studio
www.westsidestudio.com
Representative: Carolyn Somlo
www.somlotalent.com

Simmons, Tim
12A Perseverance Works
38 Kingsland Road
London E2 8DD
United Kingdom
phone: (44) 20 77 29 02 34
email: tim@timsimmons.co.uk
www.timsimmons.co.uk
Representative: Morgan Lockyer
www.morganlockyer.com
Representative: Christa Klubert
www.christaklubert.com

Simpson, Garry
email: garry@garrysimpson.com
www.garrysimpson.com
Representative: Vue
Unit 1 & 2 Elm Court, Royal Oak Yard
London SE1 3TP
United Kingdom
phone: (44) 20 74 03 55 55
fax: (44) 20 74 03 20 05

Skelton, Mike
122 Beattie Street, Balmain
Sydney, NSW 2041
Australia
phone: (61) 2 98 10 65 55
fax: (61) 2 95 55 13 56
email: mike@skelton.biz
www.skelton.biz

Smári
P.O. Box 234
Lexington, MA 02421
USA
phone: (1) 781 6 46 01 48
email: mail@smariproductions.com
www.smariproductions.com
Representative: @radical.media
http://photo.radicalmedia.com

Smetana, Andreas
P.O. Box 7016, Alexandria
Sydney, NSW 2015
Australia
phone: (61) 2 96 99 81 99
email: andreas@smetana.net
Representative Australia: Rachel Henderson
www.smetana.net
Representative USA: Marge Casey
www.margecasey.com

Smit, Boudewijn
c/o Frans Kuypers
De Beeringen 37
6681 JG Bemmel
The Netherlands
phone 1: (31) 481 48 83 88
phone 2: (31) 653 14 28 88
fax: (31) 481 48 83 89
email: office@franskuypers.com
www.franskuypers.com

Index to Photographers

Smith, Chris Frazer
5b Blackstock Mews
London N4 2BT
United Kingdom
phone: (44) 20 73 59 49 61
fax: (44) 20 72 26 85 04
email: chris@chrisfrazersmith.com
www.chrisfrazersmith.com
Representative UK: John Wyatt-Clarke
phone: (44) 20 74 86 09 99
www.wyattclarke.com
Representative France: Laurence Bonduel
phone: (33) 1 56 33 43 02
Representative USA: Anderson Hopkins
phone: (1) 212 4 31 51 17
Representative Hong Kong: The Hive
phone: (852) 34 27 52 05

Smith, Richard Hamilton
17456 Half Moon Road
Park Rapids, MN 56470
USA
phone: (1) 218 73 26 00
fax: (1) 218 73 26 26
email: studio@richardhamiltonsmith.com
www.richardhamiltonsmith.com

Stahlie, Jaap
Stuurmankade 304
1019 WD Amsterdam
The Netherlands
phone: (31) 20 4 19 81 84
fax: (31) 20 4 19 81 85
email: jaap@jaapstahlie.com
www.jaapstahlie.com

Stallaert, Kurt
c/o Frans Kuypers
De Beeringen 37
6681 JG Bemmel
The Netherlands
phone 1: (31) 481 48 83 88
phone 2: (31) 653 14 28 88
fax: (31) 481 48 83 89
email: office@franskuypers.com
www.franskuypers.com

Staudinger+Franke
Mollardgasse 85a/1/4
1060 Vienna
Austria
phone: (43) 1 5 97 01 24
email: sf@staudinger-franke.at
www.staudinger-franke.at
Representative: Marge Casey
www.margecasey.com

Stewart, David
39, Featherstone Street
London EC1Y 8RE
United Kingdom
phone: (44) 20 76 08 24 37
email: david@davidstewwwart.com
www.davidstewwwart.com
Representative: Noelle Pickford
www.noelpickford.com
Representative: Monaco Reps
www.monacoreps.com
Representative: Stefanie Diegelmann
www.sd-photo.de
Representative: Maureen Sale
www.maureensale.com

Stock, Simon
phone: (44) 20 89 50 76 79
email: simon@simonstock.com
www.simonstock.com
Representative UK: Burnham Niker
phone: (44) 20 77 04 65 65
www.burnham-niker.com
Representative USA: Greenhouse Reps
phone: (1) 212 7 04 43 00
www.greenhousereps.com
Representative Europe: g.s.abroad
phone: (44) 208 87 49 16 31
www.gsabroad.com

Stoll, Christian
144 Montague Street
Brooklyn, NY 11201
USA
phone: (1) 917 7 54 06 56
email: info@christian-stoll.com
Representative: Bransch
www.bransch.net

Stothart, Fergus
Calle Sant Elm 59
8003 Barcelona
Spain
phone: (34) 6 39 37 54 54
email: fergus@shock-studio.com
www.shock-studio.com
Representative: Gotfilm
www.gotfilm.tv

Stratmann, Rainer
Jahnstr. 6
65719 Hofheim-Lorsbach
Germany
phone: (49) 172 6 70 78 12
email: mail@rainerstratmann.com
www.rainerstratmann.com
Representative USA: Shelly Steichen
www.steichenrepresents.com

Szeling
160 Paya Lebar Road #06-09, Orion Industrial Building
Singapore 409022
Singapore
phone: (65) 96 82 30 51
fax: (65) 67 48 18 53
email: szeling@szeling.com
www.szeling.com
Representative: The Hive
www.thehive.hk
Representative: Floresco Productions
www.florescoproductions.com

Tacevski, Goran
U Nikolajky 29
150 00 Praha 5
Czech Republic
phone: (420) 251 566 117 9
email: goran@tacevski.com
www.tacevski.com
Representative Praha: Lukas Keclik
lukas@tacevski.com
Representative Paris: L'Agence VU, David Bault
bault@abvent.fr

Tacevski, Nikola
Uruguayska 5
120 00 Prague 2
Czech Republic
phone: (420) 602 31 06 01
fax: (420) 22 2 52 13 83
email: photo@tacevskinikola.com
www.tacevskinikola.com
Representative: Daiben Photographers' Agency
www.daiben.cz

Tajima, Kazunali
10-14-203 Sarugakucho, Shibuya-ku
Tokyo 150-0033
Japan
phone: (81) 3 34 64 83 10
email: contact@mildinc.com
www.tajimakazunali.com
Representative: Mild Inc.
www.mildinc.com

Taras, Seth
Los Angeles, New York
USA
phone: (1) 917 301 97 77
email: seth@sethtaras.com
www.sethtaras.com
Representative: Elizabeth Poje
www.elizabethpoje.com

Tay, Jonathan
16 Kallang Place #06-34
Singapore 339156
Singapore
phone: (65) 90 93 31 11
fax: (65) 62 97 83 62
email: jontay@jonathantay.com
www.jonathantay.com
Representative: Jaslyn Loh
jaslyn@jonathantay.com
Representative: Marge Casey
www.margecasey.com

Telfer, Alex
phone: (44) 19 12 65 73 84
email: peter@telfer-photography.com
www.alextelferphotography.com

Teo, Chai Guan
c/o Teo Studio
315 Outram Road #04-01 Tan Boon Liat Bldg.
Singapore 169074
Singapore
phone: (65) 6 3 24 63 23
fax: (65) 6 3 24 50 57
email: teostd@singnet.com.sg
www.teostudio.com.sg

Thomas, Christopher
Thalkirchnerstr. 143
81371 Munich
Germany
phone: (49) 89 7 23 45 16
fax: (49) 89 7 24 28 68
email: mail@christopher-thomas.de
www.christopher-thomas.de
Representative: Dagmar Staudenmaier
email: welcome@staudenmaier.de
Representative: Imaginativ
email: imaginat@imaginativ.com
Representative: Jean Gardner
email: jean@jgaonline.com

Tsubaki, Takashi
1-17-100 Minami-Aoyama Minato-ku
Tokyo 107-0062
Japan
phone: (81) 3 57 45 00 68
fax: (81) 3 57 45 00 69
email: miyumiya@za.bb-east.ne.jp

Turnley, Gerard
P.O. Box 657
1684 Kyalami Estate
South Africa
phone: (27) 11 4 68 29 12
email: gerard@turnleyphoto.com
www.turnleyphoto.com
Representative: Imaginativ
www.imaginativ.com
Representative: PhotographersCOACH
www.photographerscoach.com

van den Berg, Jo
Holstenstr. 110
22767 Hamburg
Germany
phone: (49) 40 38 16 48
fax: (49) 40 3 89 48 17
email: info@jovandenberg.com
www.jovandenberg.com

van der Hulst, René
Molenbochtplein 33
5014 EJ Tilburg
The Netherlands
phone: (31) 13 5 43 53 54
email: rene@renevanderhulst.nl
www.renevanderhulst.nl
Representative: Galahad
www.galahad.nl

van der Lugt, Gerdjan
Palamedesstraat 6
1054 HS Amsterdam
The Netherlands
phone: (31) 20 6 07 15 15
fax: (31) 20 6 07 15 00
email: gerdjan@shootings.com
www.shootings.com
Representative: Witman Kleinpool
[illegible]
Representative: Silvia Koelliker
www.silviakoelliker.com

van der Vlugt, Marcel
c/o Frans Kuypers
De Beeringen 37
6681 JG Bemmel
The Netherlands
phone 1: (31) 481 48 83 88
phone 2: (31) 653 14 28 88
fax: (31) 481 48 83 89
email: office@franskuypers.com
www.franskuypers.com

van Overbeek, Will
[illegible] Ridgeview
[illegible], TX [illegible]
USA
phone: (1) 512 [illegible]
email: studio@willvano.com
www.willvano.com

van Velzen, Joris
Russia:
Ul. Vavilova 65a, Studio 710
117292 Moscow
phone: (7) 495 7 28 69 24
Germany:
Am Tempelhofer Berg 6
10965 Berlin
phone: (49) 177 25 34 803
email: info@jorisvanvelzen.com
www.jorisvanvelzen.com

Vedros, Nick
1510 Jarboe
Kansas City, MO 66208
USA
phone: (1) 816 4 71 54 88
fax: (1) 816 4 71 26 66
email: nick.vedros@vedros.com
www.vedros.com
Representative: Cathy Kudelko
www.vedros.com
Representative: Lisa Button – Chicago, Dallas & Minneapolis Rep
www.buttonrepresents.com

Veltman, Olaf
c/o Frans Kuypers
De Beeringen 37
6681 JG Bemmel
The Netherlands
phone 1: (31) 481 48 83 88
phone 2: (31) 653 14 28 88
fax: (31) 481 48 83 89
email: office@franskuypers.com
www.franskuypers.com

Viitala, Antti
Bulevardi 19D 31
00120 Helsinki
Finland
phone: (358) 500 50 00 87
email: peikko@anttiviitala.com
www.anttiviitala.com
Representative: Celeste Horn
www.oneleague.co.za

Vilela, Leonardo
Rua do Catete 92, Casa 19
Rio de Janeiro, RJ 22220 000
Brazil
phone: (55) 21 22 25 72 24
fax: (55) 21 22 25 72 25
email: leovilela@platinumfmd.com.br
www.platinumfmd.com.br
Representative USA: Charlie Holtz
www.[illegible]
Representative Europe: [illegible]
www.artwareindustry.com

Vliegenthart, Jaap
Bolstroen 20
1046 AT Amsterdam
The Netherlands
phone: (31) 20 4 11 77 35
fax: (31) 20 6 14 54 96
email: info@jaapvliegenthart.nl
www.jaapvliegenthart.nl
Representative: Maria Calheiros
www.mariacalheiros.com
Representative: Unit C.M.A.
www.unit.nl

von [illegible]
47 B Keele St [illegible]
Melbourne, Victoria 3066
Australia
phone 1: (61) 3 94 17 00 50
phone 2: (61) 412 99 91 15
email: chris@chrisvon.com
www.chrisvon.com

von Renner, Ivo
Metzendorfer Weg 11
21224 Rosengarten
Germany
phone: (49) 4108 43 30 00
email: mail@ivofolio.com
www.ivofolio.com

Vonier, Julien
Binzstr. 39
8045 Zurich
Switzerland
phone: (41) 44 4 63 80 10
fax: (41) 44 4 63 80 34
email: vonier@vonier.ch
www.vonier.ch

Warmer, Simon
Dukdalfweg 38
1041 BE Amsterdam
The Netherlands
phone: (31) 20 6 92 39 55
fax: (31) 20 6 93 15 11
email: simon@simonwarmer.nl
www.simonwarmer.nl

Watanabe, Hajime
#401 Minami-Azabu 4-2-49, Minato-ku
Tokyo 106-0047
Japan
phone: (81) 3 34 48 11 39
email: hajime@hwphotography.com
www.hwphotography.com
www.a-hum.org
Representative: Kayoko Sato
www.kayokosato.com

Watts, Anthony
The Power Station, Coronet Street
London N1 6HD
United Kingdom
phone: (44) 20 77 39 86 78
fax: (44) 20 77 39 84 89
emai: anton@antonwatts.com
www.antonwatts.com
Representative: Catherine Collins
www.catherinecollins.co.uk
Representative: Anderson Hopkins
www.andersonhopkins.com

Wexler, Glen
736 North Highland Avenue
Los Angeles, CA 90038
USA
phone: (1) 323 4 65 02 68
email: info@glenwexler.com
www.glenwexler.com

Whitman, Robert
63 Downing #9B
New York, NY 10014
USA
phone: (1) 646 3 36 71 67
email: robert@robertwhitman.com
www.robertwhitman.com
Representative: Greenhouse Reps
www.greenhousereps.com

Wilson, Robert
70 Shaftesbury Road
London N19 4QN
United Kingdom
phone: (44) 20 72 63 99 01
email: robert@robertjwilson.com
www.robertjwilson.com
Representative: Catherine Collins
www.catherinecollins.co.uk

Winkler & Noah
Via Laurentina [illegible]
00143 Rome
Italy
phone: (39) 06 45 49 09 85
fax: (39) 06 45 49 09 84
email: wn@winkler-noah.it
www.winkler-noah.it
Representative Italy: Mandala CP
www.mandalacp.it
Representative Spain: First Factory
www.firstfactory.net
Representative Eastern Europe: Umbrela
www.umbrela.ro

Wlazly, Adam
Dobra 53/62
00-312 Warsaw
Poland
email: adam@alabama.pl
www.alabama.pl
Representative: Malgosia Byliniak
email: malgosiabyliniak@alabama.pl

Wunsche, Magda
email: mail@magdawunsche.com
www.magdawunsche.com

YangTan
Representative: Monaco Reps
44 West 18th Street
8th Floor, Suite D
New York, NY 10011
USA
phone: (1) 212 647 03 36
www.monacoreps.com

Zibert, Mark
17 Carlaw Avenue Unit 5
Toronto M4M 2R6
Canada
phone (1) 414 69 49 00
email: mark@methodinc.net
www.markzibert.com
Representative: Jooli Kim
www.jkreps.com
Representative: Corbis Assignment
www.corbis.com/zibert

Ziviani, Fernando
Av. Candido Hartmann 5248
Curitiba, PR 82015-100
Brazil
phone: (55) 41 30 27 72 73
email: ziviani@ziviani.com
www.ziviani.com

Alphabetical Index A-M